August Wilson: Pittsburgh Places
in His Life and Plays

A Pennsylvania Historical and Museum Commission marker designates August Wilson's birthplace and childhood home at 1727 Bedford Avenue in Pittsburgh's Hill District.

August Wilson:
Pittsburgh Places
in His Life and Plays

Laurence A. Glasco and Christopher Rawson

Pittsburgh History & Landmarks Foundation

Pittsburgh History & Landmarks Foundation
100 West Station Square Drive, Suite 450
Pittsburgh, PA 15219-1134
412-471-5808
www.phlf.org

ISBN 978-0-9788284-7-9
Library of Congress Control Number: 2010940939

Laurence A. Glasco and Christopher Rawson, *Authors*
Louise King Sturgess, *Project director/editor*
Albert M. Tannler, *Co-editor*
Greg Pytlik of Pytlik Design Associates, Inc., *Designer*

August Wilson: Pittsburgh Places in His Life and Plays is typeset
in Minion with Formata. It was printed on 80# Genuine Silk Text
by Migliozzi Printing Services and Knepper Press Corporation,
Clinton, PA.

*This guidebook has been financed in part with Federal funds from
the National Park Service, U.S. Department of the Interior. However,
the contents and opinions do not necessarily reflect the views or policies
of the Department of the Interior.*

Cover photo: November 18, 1999. August Wilson in front of the New
Granada Theater in Pittsburgh's Hill District, 2007 Centre Avenue.

Contributors

This guidebook is supported by a Preserve America grant from the National Park Service, administered under the Preserving African American Heritage in Pennsylvania program of the Pennsylvania Historical and Museum Commission.

Lead Donors

BNY Mellon Foundation of Southwestern Pennsylvania

Multicultural Arts Initiative

Walter C. Kidney Library and Publications Fund, Pittsburgh History & Landmarks Foundation

Patrons

Alfred M. Oppenheimer Memorial Fund of The Pittsburgh Foundation

Mr. & Mrs. Charles H. Booth, Jr.

Harry C. Goldby

Grambrindi Davies Charitable Fund of The Pittsburgh Foundation

The Heinz Endowments

Hugh and Eliza Nevin

Dr. Howard B. Slaughter, Jr., and Mrs. Janet A. Slaughter

Partners

Anonymous (2)

Audrey and Kenneth Menke Fund for Education, Pittsburgh History & Landmarks Foundation

Jennifer Ayers

Jeanne B. Berdik

Claudia Bermudez

Mr. & Mrs. Harold L. Blye

Carl Wood Brown

Karen and Mike Cahall

Barry Chad

Mary and John Davis

Sally and James Dawson

Mary Lu and Jim Denny, in memory of Dom Magasano

Leroy and Gwen Dillard

(continued)

Partners (continued)

Lu and E. J. Donnelly

Robert A. Ehrman

Senator Jim Ferlo

Dr. & Mrs. William S. Garrett, Jr.

Joan and Stuart Gaul

Philip B. Hallen

Henry P. Hoffstot, Jr.

William C. and Virginia A. Keck

Mr. & Mrs. William C. King

David Kleer

Stanley A. Lowe

Emma T. Lucas-Darby, PhD

Manchester Citizens
Corporation Board of Directors

Sara McGuire

Shaunda Miles

Mary Anne and Bill Mistick

E. O'Neill and Brunetti Family

Trevi and Ray Pendro

Marylynne Pitz

Curtiss E. Porter, PhD

Marirose and John Radelet

Matthew J. Ragan

Dorothy and Nicholas Rescher

Anne Robb

Dr. & Mrs. Wilfred T. Rouleau

Ann Fay Ruben

Louise and Martin Sturgess

Kathy and Lou Testoni

David J. Vater

Carol Yaster and
William Levant

This gigapanorama, taken from the roof of the U.S. Steel Tower on October 19, 2009, shows the Hill District—made famous in August Wilson's Pittsburgh Cycle of plays—rising east of downtown Pittsburgh. The Allegheny River (left) and Monongahela River (right) have been in their present courses for some 12,000 years, and the hills are some 300 million years old. The Monongahela River is mentioned in three of August Wilson's plays: *Gem of the Ocean*, *Joe Turner's Come and Gone*, and *Two Trains Running*. The dome-shaped Civic Arena (now vacant) and the Consol Energy Center (right) are the most prominent structures in the Lower Hill.

Looking east on Bedford Avenue in Pittsburgh's Hill District. This is
the street where August Wilson lived from 1945 to 1958. At the time,
other black families, Italians, Jews, Greeks, and Syrians lived up and
down the street. Eight buildings remain in this handsome row of brick
Romanesque Revival houses, a style brought to the Pittsburgh area
by German immigrants.

Contents

Introduction xi
  Pride and Pain of Place xiii
  Growing Up with August xvii

The Playwright and His Hometown 1
  August Wilson: The Ground on Which He Stood 3
  The Hill and the African American Experience 29

Guide 57
  Hill District Map 58
  Hill District Tour 61
  Pittsburgh Area Map 100
  Tour of Sites Beyond the Hill 103

Appendices 119
  The Pittsburgh Cycle: Summaries 121
  Acknowledgments 129
  Illustration Sources 133
  Bibliography 135
  Index 139

RUBY: I know where I'm at. I know I'm
in Pittsburgh. I done seen lots of
cities before. They may not have
been up North, but a city is a city.
It don't make no difference.

FLOYD: Sure it do. This is Pittsburgh.
This ain't Alabama. Some things
you get away with up here you
can't get away with down there.
I'll show you around. It ain't as
good as Chicago, but you be
surprised at what you find.

—*Seven Guitars*: Act Two, Scene 1

1951: The Lower Hill and downtown Pittsburgh, with the first U.S.
Steel Building (now 525 William Penn Place) under construction
(rising behind the church spire) and the Gulf Building (right),
the tallest in Pittsburgh at the time. The Gulf Building and Gulf
Oil Company are mentioned in two of August Wilson's plays,
Two Trains Running and *Jitney*, and are more important in
The Piano Lesson.

Introduction

What I want to do is place the culture of black America on stage, to demonstrate that it has the ability to offer sustenance, so that when you leave your parents' house, you are not in the world alone. You have something that is yours, you have a ground to stand on, and you have a viewpoint, and you have a way of proceeding in the world that has been developed by your ancestors.

CONVERSATIONS WITH AUGUST WILSON:
"AUGUST WILSON: AN INTERVIEW,"
VERA SHEPPARD, 1990

Pride and Pain of Place

Kimberly C. Ellis, PhD

The historic Hill District is a special place that has captured the imagination of the world. Students from as far away as Kenya, Beijing, and London have explored the works of August Wilson and fallen in love with the characters, the place, and the spirit of Hill residents in a manner unprecedented. The exploration and celebration of place, of community and everyday people, is what makes August Wilson's creative focus upon the Hill District such a specifically renowned accomplishment.

Why is place so important? What is it about the ways in which we build community—a combination of the built environment and the persons who populate it—that means so much to us? How is it that neatly laid concrete and carefully spaced trees can harness, externally, the interior hopes and dreams stacked inside of a brick row house on a slanted street? Why does it matter that a demolished building with abruptly broken sidewalks, a disjointed porch and crumbling steps is not only a monument to a certain lack of care and concern, but also a testament to the inevitability of change?

Our places are important to us because they are what we have, at any given time, as human beings grappling with meaning for ourselves, our lives, and each other. We build community with our wants, our needs, and our imaginations long before the first blueprint is created; and community remains in our memories long after the bulldozers have rolled away. What August Wilson did in setting the majority of his plays in the Hill District was to capture the essence of its spirit and display the universal qualities of humanity—in a century of African American life. But, although he grew up in Pittsburgh, he found he could not live here, anymore.

In her essay, "The Place Where I Was Born," Alice Walker writes, "As a child I assumed I would always have the middle Georgia landscape to live in, as Br'er Rabbit, a native also, and relative, had his brier patch. It was not to be. The pain of racist oppression, and its consequence, economic impoverishment, drove me to the four corners of the earth in search of justice and peace, and work that affirmed my whole being."

For August Wilson, Pittsburgh was a source of pride and pain and the place he sought to visit, only, because, like Walker, he needed to live in places that affirmed his whole being. The historic Hill District, its peoples and their narratives, stand as a testament to the resilience, depth of culture, and sheer force of will to survive, too often in spite of what the city has to offer in terms of employment, housing, and entrepreneurial and social opportunities.

As a child, I grew up watching the man (whom the world would know with increasing fascination as "August Wilson") come and go from my mother's home: she was his eldest sister. Freda Ellis's house on Bedford Avenue became the center of all of the family gatherings, since it was close to 1621 Bedford Avenue, where August's mother, Daisy Wilson, lived (see page 68). After Daisy passed and her house sat empty, with boarded up windows and doors, the family continued to gather in the Hill, annually in March, in her memory. Rather than stay in hotels, the family members who lived outside of the city piled up—in what were neither spacious nor grand accommodations—on extra beds, sofas, and homemade cots and pallets, just to remain close with one another. It was also easy access to my mother's good cooking, late-night board games and card-playing, storytelling, laughter, and the sharing of memories. August seemed to particularly enjoy this arrangement, especially as a young man and continuing as his star kept rising. Many of the names and places which showed up in his plays were actually family members and places we'd visited; so we reminisced about them with the entire family, at the Ellis house.

"Pittsburgh Memories," 1984, by Romare Bearden. August Wilson said, "my four Bs—Bearden, Baraka, Borges, blues ... are the major influences in my life." Bearden's collage, "The Piano Lesson," inspired Wilson's play by that name, and his "Mill Hand's Lunch Bucket" inspired *Joe Turner's Come and Gone.*

Collage on board, H: 73 x W: 60 cm.
Art © Romare Bearden Foundation/
Licensed by VAGA, New York, NY

The importance of place and the meaning of culture and humanity, as well as the looming presence of one's mortality, is captured for me in Romare Bearden's collage, "Pittsburgh Memories": the façade of a row house (with smokestacks in the distance) is cut away to reveal a family inhabiting life together, in all of its multifaceted glory and complications.

In his plays, August Wilson offers the world a vision of black life and human life that can give each of us something that is ours, "a ground to stand on ... a way of proceeding in the world that has been developed by your ancestors." He gives voice to bricks and mortar and shows the world what it means to stand, stone-faced, against anything that chooses to devalue one's humanity. This is why the world loves the place that August Wilson built and why the historic Hill District remains ensconced in the hearts and minds of all who encounter its community. It is our hope that you will come to love the Hill with even greater depth and understanding, once you arrive in this special place. □

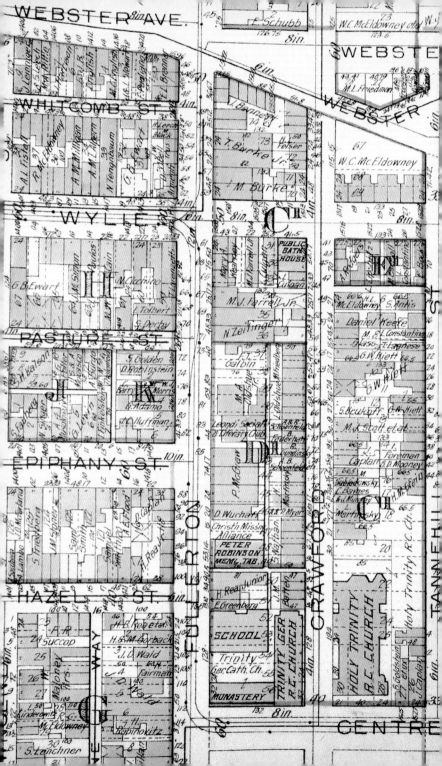

Growing Up with August

Sala Udin

I met August Wilson—then Freddy Kittel—at Holy Trinity School on Fullerton Street in Pittsburgh's Hill District around 1952; August was seven years old, I was two years older.

My family converted to Roman Catholicism and, because my mother did house cleaning for the Holy Trinity Parish, we did not pay tuition to attend school, but August's mother, Daisy Wilson, probably paid for him to attend. Because there were few black students at Holy Trinity, we stuck together and formed lasting friendships. Neighborhood kids saw nuns and priests as "spooky"—they never married, they had very white faces, and were dressed in black. But, we students retorted, "We got a good education. We learned to speak proper English!" August would never raise his hand in class to give the answer; but, if a nun called on him, he usually knew the answer. He was shy … he didn't participate in football or rough physical games in the schoolyard, but he always watched, with a sly smile on his face.

Kids can make a playground out of anything—Oatmeal boxes become footballs, a broomstick becomes a baseball bat. You could be poor but still have fun and that's the way we lived in the Lower Hill. My family lived at the corner of Fullerton and Epiphany streets. The buildings were old and decrepit and the winters were hard—but that was winter. We all knew each other. We played together outside in the spring and summer. We were safe and well taken care of.

Then a rumor started to creep through the Lower Hill that everyone was going to have to move because they were going to tear down the whole neighborhood. To kids, this was frightening. Will I have a new school? Will I have to find new friends? Why are they tearing our neighborhood down? Why not just fix it up? All of our questions were happening outside of our control. Everyone we knew was a victim. It was happening to them. Holy Trinity School was slated for demolition and we were told we had to transfer to St. Richard's School on Bedford Avenue.

Then, my parents were rather suddenly told we had been awarded a place in Bedford Dwellings, a public housing project that was being expanded. Mom and Dad were happy. Okay. That allayed our fears. Around 1953, we moved on the weekend. I was ten years old. Once we started moving in, we saw a lot of the people we knew from "Down the Hill." (That's how we referred to the Lower Hill.) That made it easier. We got a brand new kitchen: never seen *brand new* before—with all the appliances a family could want. Then we learned that heating and electricity were included in the rent. To be warm in the winter—that was something, that was amazing—an indescribable feeling when you had known bitter cold. As more people moved in over the course of the next couple of weeks, our circle of friends grew. Bedford Dwellings became a great place to live. August's family lived on Bedford Avenue, above the demolition, but a rumor persisted that demolition would spread. His mother moved the family to Hazelwood in 1958, but he came back to live in the Hill as a young man.

As I grew older, I came to understand that the policy of the city's housing redevelopment authority was racist, consciously segregating the community. While blacks were moved into public housing, federal government home loans and grants to poor white families facilitated white flight by giving them the means to move into neighborhoods that they otherwise couldn't afford to live in and establish themselves as homeowners.

As young adults, August and I and others became a political movement—some of us worked in politics, some worked for access to the University of Pittsburgh, some worked against segregation in public schools, some fought drug abuse, and some worked in the arts. The arts were integrated into our political meetings. They might open the meeting or close the meeting; sometimes the arts *were* the meeting. But we were political activists *first* and art was a tool of our activism. Poetry helped bring an otherwise boring political meeting to life. Once we began emphasizing our African heritage, we added African drums and singers to the art that was integrated into the politics.

August started writing poetry. Poets were important leaders in the Black Power movement. They were the flame throwers. They were highly revered and highly influential, starting from 1964 on, especially Amiri Baraka, whom August admired. The formative years of August Wilson, the playwright, were from 1965 through 1978, here in Pittsburgh.

August, Rob Penny, myself, and others started the Black Horizon Theater in 1968. I was the lead actor. We paid for the Black Horizon Theater out of our pockets—the costumes, stage sets, etc. We produced these plays with our own money. We were so spent and broke that, when Dr. Vernell Lillie opened Kuntu Repertory Theatre in 1975, we said PHEW!— now we can quit, now we can let it go.

Leaving Pittsburgh created a dilemma for August—we never forgave Claude Purdy for taking him away!—but leaving fed August, refreshed him, and released him. In St. Paul, he was meeting new people, rising to the top. He loved to come back and talk with Rob Penny and me about his exploits.

August was a "thought leader." It always amazed me how he was wise enough to see in this poor, depleted ghetto neighborhood a subject for serious theater; how he could see that our broken English was right and pure for the stage. □

RUBY: ... That's the longest hill I ever
seen. I can't be walking up these
hills getting all them muscles in
my legs.

CANEWELL: For your information, in case
you ain't figured it out yourself, this
here is called the Hill District.

—*SEVEN GUITARS*: ACT ONE, SCENE 5

1953: Framed by the first Alcoa Building downtown,
Pittsburgh's Lower Hill rises steeply beyond, all the
way up to its eastern end marked by the radio
tower and U.S. Veterans Administration Hospital,
completed in 1954.

The Playwright and His Hometown

August Wilson: The Ground on Which He Stood

Christopher Rawson

Award-winning playwright August Wilson was born in 1945 in Pittsburgh's Hill District, where he grew up and matured his artist's vision. In 1978, not quite thirty-three, he moved to St. Paul, Minnesota, and in 1990 to Seattle, Washington, where he died suddenly in 2005, just sixty.

During his lifetime, he became not only a familiar presence on Broadway but also a leading citizen of the national theater, rewriting and staging his plays throughout the United States. But it is the Hill of Wilson's youth and young adulthood that remained the deep well of memory into which he kept dipping the ladle of his art. To visit his family and friends, and also to revisit that past, he kept coming back, both in memory and in person, as he said, "to reconnect with Pittsburgh ... this is fertile ground."

Wilson used history much as Shakespeare did, as raw material in which to locate his themes, the "love, honor, duty and betrayal" that he claimed were at the heart of all his plays. The Hill and his creative imagination provided the rich stream of stories, images, and conflicts with which, in plays set in each decade of the twentieth century, he dramatized the comedy and tragedy, thwarted passions and visionary aspirations of a century of African American history and culture.

The Hill was such fertile ground that he set nine of his ten plays in its homes, offices, shops, streets, and dusty backyards. Asked why one of the plays, *Ma Rainey's Black Bottom*, is set in Chicago, he said, "It was my first play [on Broadway] and

November 18, 1999: August Wilson at 1727 Bedford Avenue; his childhood home was the two-room apartment up the stairs in the rear (see page 70).

I was from Pittsburgh, so I thought I needed a more important city"—a typical Pittsburgh attitude. Even for his second Broadway play, *Fences*, the original Playbill read simply, "a northern industrial city," which, its director Lloyd Richards said, "one might correctly mistake for Pittsburgh," since it breathes Pittsburgh in every reference and place name. But for all his plays to follow, the Playbill read, "Pittsburgh, the Hill District." This is why his extraordinary ten-play epic is best called the Pittsburgh Cycle (a name for which he gave tacit permission). In the cycle he created August Wilson's Hill District, a real world of the imagination to rank with such other famous fictionalized real worlds as William Faulkner's Yoknapatawpha County, Thomas Hardy's Wessex, or Brian Friel's Donegal.

Critics from Manhattan to Los Angeles now speak know-ingly of "Pittsburgh's Hill." This is not the Hill as it actually is today or even as it was when Wilson grew up there in the 1950s and 1960s, but an archetypal northern urban black neighborhood, evolving over both historic and imaginative time, a construct of frustration, nostalgia, anger, and dream. The real Hill was once a city within a city, with a proud history of art, sports, and journalism. Then, it was torn apart by urban renewal in the 1950s and by the fires of 1968. Now, as if in cosmic compensation, the Hill lives on in Wilson's imagination. But it is also real, with a history of vibrant life and tragic death, struggling to revive the vital community it once was.

The plays are also about people, based partly on those Wilson knew in the Hill, partly on his imagination, and ultimately on himself. In 1988, he told Bill Moyers in a television interview, "I get so immersed in [my plays] that as I'm inventing this world, I'm also becoming a part of it. You discover that you're walking down this landscape of the self. ... Gabriel is me. Rose is a part of myself. Corey, Troy, Loomis, Levy, and Toledo—they're all different aspects of the self."

David Gallo's evocative stage set for Chicago's Goodman Theatre, later recreated for the 2007 Broadway premiere of *Radio Golf* at the Cort Theatre. The action takes place in 1997 in Harmond Wilks' redevelopment office on Centre Avenue (center). The ghostly, derelict barbershop (left) and diner (right) are silent time capsules of the Hill in its livelier days, evoking the communal arenas of tale-telling and friendship that August Wilson celebrated and lamented in his plays.

Starting in 1984, the Pittsburgh Cycle plays swept through the American theater. All ten enjoyed high-profile runs in New York, our theatrical heartland—nine opened on Broadway (*Jitney* excepted), where there is now a theater named the August Wilson. But all ten have found their most appreciative audiences in that other American heartland, the large not-for-profit professional theaters in every major city. The last of the ten plays had its Broadway debut in 2007, two years after Wilson died, but by then, the earlier plays were already enjoying major revivals, which continue today.

Rich in both humor and pain, powered by expressive language and poignant story, the plays have already become classics of the American stage. Each stands alone, but together, as the Pittsburgh Cycle, they are unmatched in American theater for scope and cumulative effect. Wilson has taken his place as a great American playwright alongside Eugene O'Neill, Tennessee Williams, Arthur Miller, and Edward Albee.

Pittsburgh Youth

All this was an extraordinary achievement for a man born April 27, 1945, in the poorest of circumstances at 1727 Bedford Avenue. Wilson commented on this when he accepted *Pittsburgh Magazine*'s Pittsburgher of the Year award in 1990, rooting his accomplishments in the struggles of his ancestors:

> I was born in Pittsburgh in 1945 and for thirty-three years stumbled through its streets, small, narrow, crooked, cobbled, with the weight of the buildings pressing in on me and my spirit pushed into terrifying contractions. That I would stand before you today in this guise was beyond comprehension .... I am standing here in my grandfather's shoes. ... They are the shoes of a whole generation of men who left a life of unspeakable horror in the South and came North ... searching for jobs, for the opportunity to live a life with dignity and whatever eloquence the heart could call upon. ... The cities were not then, and are not now, hospitable. There is a struggle to maintain one's dignity. But that generation of men and women stands as a testament to the resiliency of the human spirit. And they have passed on to us, their grand-children, the greatest of gifts, the gift of hope refreshened.

Wilson was born Frederick August Kittel, the fourth child of seven and the first boy, which is why he was given his father's name. His father was a German immigrant and talented baker, but, according to August, he wasn't around much; he died in 1965. Wilson was called Freddy as a child and his family continued to call him Freddy all his life, even after he became famous as the playwright August Wilson. His mother, Daisy Wilson, whose own mother, Zonia, had walked north to Pittsburgh from North Carolina, raised her children in a cold-water flat behind Bella's Market on Bedford Avenue. She died of lung cancer in March 1983, just before her son's first great success on Broadway, but after he had started to show the creative talent that would get him there.

"My father very rarely came around," Wilson said, with studied understatement. "I grew up in my mother's household in a cultural environment which was black." He also had a black stepfather, David Bedford, who died in 1969. Wilson's older sisters, Freda, Linda Jean, and Donna, and his younger brothers, Edwin and Richard, all survived him. Another sister, Barbara, was raised by relatives. His brothers kept their father's name, but at twenty, just after his father died, the future playwright signaled his cultural loyalty by becoming August Wilson, taking his mother's name, showing where he located his cultural roots.

Wilson remembered that his mother "had a very hard time feeding us all. But I had a wonderful childhood. … As a family, we did things together. We said the rosary every night at seven o'clock. We all sat down and had dinner at a certain time. … We didn't have a TV, so we listened to the radio."

One of his mother's enduring gifts was to teach him to read when he was four years old. Wilson called it transforming: "You can unlock information and you're better able to understand the forces that are oppressing you." Years later he recounted at a library celebration, "I got my first library card from the Hill District branch of Carnegie Library on Wylie Avenue in 1950. Labor historians do not speak well of Andrew Carnegie … [but he] will forever be for me that man who made it possible for me to stand here today. … I wore out my library card and cried when I lost it."

There was another library memory. After the family moved

to Hazelwood in 1958, he walked one day into the local Carnegie Library branch, with a basketball under his arm, and discovered a shelf marked "Negro Books." There were only thirty or forty books, and he read them all. He remembered wanting to see "my book up there, too. I used to dream about being part of the Harlem Renaissance."

His mother valued education. She started him in the Pittsburgh Public Schools at Letsche, but then enrolled him in parochial schools, first Holy Trinity and then St. Richard's—both in the Hill—and then, when the family moved to Hazelwood, in St. Stephen's. The family was not Roman Catholic, but his mother saw the value of Catholic schools and religious traditions such as saying the rosary as a family. And, as a young child, Wilson had been gathered up with other children by a neighborhood woman, Sarah Degree (a name that appears in three of his plays). As he told an interviewer, "We started going to church with Miss Sarah."

After graduating from the eighth grade at St. Stephen's, he enrolled in 1959 at Central Catholic High School in Oakland. As the only black student in his ninth-grade homeroom, Freddy Kittel was constantly taunted and harassed. This led to fights and many days when he was sent home early, so he left Central Catholic just before the end of the school year. The next fall he started back in the Hill at Connelley vocational school, which he found pointless. The teachers accused him of being careless with the tools, which they seemed to value more than their students. He was in detention there on October 13, 1960, when the Pirates beat the Yankees at Forbes Field in nearby Oakland to win the World Series. Dismissed early, he walked through downtown Pittsburgh and saw the crowds turn over cars in jubilation as the police stood by watching—which, he noted in later years, contrasted with their very different behavior during the anti-racism and anti-war protests of the 1970s.

In early 1961, in the middle of the school year, Wilson switched to Gladstone High School, just across the street from his family's Hazelwood home. He was supposedly in the tenth grade, but because he had not graduated from ninth grade at Central Catholic, the school had him taking ninth grade subjects. He was a voracious reader, but the school work was well below his interest and abilities, so the young Wilson was bored and sat in the back of the class, observing what he described later as the school's racist expectations.

Then he realized he would want to go to college, so he decided to join the after-school college club run by one of his teachers. To show what good work he could do, he submitted a twenty-page research paper on Napoleon. In an often-told story, the teacher accused him in a classroom confrontation of having his older sisters write it for him. "I write papers for them," he said, but the teacher gave him an F. Insulted and angry, Wilson dropped the paper in a wastebasket and dropped out of school. It was right around his sixteenth birthday. He could not tell his mother what he had done, so for a while he went to school each day and shot baskets outside the principal's office, expecting someone to come out and ask why he was not in class. But no one seemed to care, and he never went back to high school.

It was "a disappointment to my mother," he recalled in another understatement, "because she wanted me to go to a nice Catholic college and be a lawyer." But as he most memorably said, "I dropped out of school but I didn't drop out of life. … I would leave the house each morning and go to the main branch of the Carnegie Library in Oakland, where they had all the books in the world. … I felt suddenly liberated from the constraints of a pre-arranged curriculum that labored through one book in eight months." That main Carnegie Library was his real high school, and, along with the streets of the Hill, his college, too.

The Hill

Meanwhile, his mother moved to Homewood, in the eastern section of the city. Wilson enlisted in the army in 1962, leaving before serving a full term. Soon his mother was back in the Hill and it was time for Wilson to declare his independence. The most important part of Wilson's education came on the streets. As he memorably put it, "I grew up without a father. When I was twenty, I went down onto Centre Avenue to learn from the community how to be a man." He told an interviewer, "Pittsburgh is a very hard city, especially if you're black," and, "When I was twenty-two years old, each day had to be continually negotiated. It was rough."

But the Hill community provided many fathers—the old men chatting in Pat's Place or on street corners; the inhabitants of the jitney stations and diners where Wilson sat and listened; or like-minded friends with artistic inclinations. He remembered, "Hanging out in the barbershop was like sitting around the fire while the tribal elders talk." His true father was both the small community that nurtured him and the larger Pittsburgh that, by opposing, stimulated and defined him.

Wilson rented a room on Crawford Street, the first of several such Hill rooms, and worked at many jobs. He discovered the blues. He followed various black identity movements and fought for social justice. And, featuring himself a poet, he sat long hours in diners, scribbling on napkins. "I always had a napkin and a pencil," he recalled. "That's one of the things about writing—the tools are so simple. At that time a lot of my friends were painters, and they were always trying to get money for paint, for canvas, and I would probably have started painting back then if I could have afforded it. But a pencil and paper were cheaper."

He remembered when he decided to be a writer. "The exact day I became a poet was April 1, 1965, the day I bought my first typewriter," using twenty dollars one of his sisters had paid him for writing a college term paper. As he told it, that was also the day he gave himself his new name, taking his typewriter back to his rented room and typing out a series of possibilities: Frederick August Kittel … Freddy Kittel … August Kittel … Frederick August Wilson … August Wilson. It is telling that his final choice includes one name from each parent.

By all accounts, Wilson's initial appearance as a young adult on the Hill was distinctive. He decided to dress himself on a poetic model, choosing the lyrical and bawdy Welsh bard, Dylan Thomas. His youthful friend Nathan Oliver, two years his senior, remembered those early years in these excerpts from a tribute poem he wrote when Wilson was dying:

He spit and sputtered his way through second-handed
Crooked-neck, hand-carved pipes, and stale tobacco

Preferred herringbone (he did) and sported British tweed
*   with its rough woolen texture*
To match his occasional abrasive manner

With omnipresent scepter and notebook he wandered
*   the avenues*
From Bedford to Five [sic] in vertical reconnaissance
Crisscrossed Crawford, Roberts, Hillman [sic],
*   Dinwiddie, DeVilliers and Kirkpatrick …*
Stranger in a grand land of hazardous hills defined
*   by asphalt dreams*

He could be annoying but brilliant a spark plug igniting
*   questions about what it meant to Be Black   what it*
*   took to become fully a man …*

He was Anthropologist and Poet.   Poet turned Playwright
Tryin' to get it right …

Yet he was August, crimson, gold, and yellow and
*   occasionally even mellow*

Wilson frequented the resale shops, such as St. Vincent de Paul and Goodwill, not just for the tweed jackets and caps that made him such a singular figure in his newly hip and Afro-centric artistic circles, but also for old 78 RPM records he bought for five cents. One day he found among them a typewritten yellow label, Bessie Smith's "Nobody in Town Can Bake a Sweet Jelly Roll Like Mine." In a story he told often, "I listened to the record twenty-two straight times. Just over and over. … It was someone speaking directly to me." As he explained, "The blues are important primarily because they contain the cultural responses of blacks in America to the situation. … I find in the music the ideas and attitudes of the characters and I dig 'em out. Music has this baptismal grace that just spills over." The blues were both cultural history and sacrament.

In the late 1960s, Wilson became part of a talented group of poets, educators, and artists of the future, young men such as Rob Penny, Nick Flournoy, "Dingbat," and Chawley Williams. The friends had regular haunts at Eddie's Restaurant, the Halfway Art Gallery, and the Hill Arts Society. In a film interview after Wilson died, Williams talked about first meeting this serious young man with his tweed jacket and cap and introducing him to other writers and artists along Centre Avenue—which is why they eventually called their writing group "Poets in the Centre Avenue Tradition." Once, it was Wylie Avenue that was the center of the black Hill; Centre Avenue had been dominated by Jews. But the blunders of urban renewal in the 1950s had demolished the commercial end of Wylie, and then the riots and fires after Martin Luther King, Jr.'s, assassination in 1968 had made the Hill increasingly black all over.

Wilson was involved in the debates of the 1960s and always considered himself "a black nationalist and a cultural nationalist." In 1969, he married Brenda Burton and they had a daughter, Sakina Ansari. That marriage ended in divorce in

1972, partly because, he said, on Sundays he was more interested in watching football on television than accompanying his wife to Black Muslim meetings.

Many years later he recalled, "The first time I became aware of theater was Pearl Bailey in *Hello, Dolly*, around 1958, 1959. My mother was in New York and brought back the program, her first and only Broadway show." His own first exposures to theater were off-putting. In 1965, he saw a thirty-minute excerpt of Eugene Ionesco's absurdist drama, *The Rhinoceros*, at Fifth Avenue High School in Pittsburgh. "That was the first theater I recall, and I wasn't impressed." He met some of the actors in John Hancock's 1966 Pittsburgh Playhouse company, but he stayed for only twenty minutes of Bertolt Brecht's *A Man's a Man*. It was 1976 before Wilson was impressed by a whole, professional play: Athol Fugard's *Sizwe Bansi Is Dead*, a comic-tragic account of life under apartheid, at the Pittsburgh Public Theater, then on the Northside.

Nonetheless, in 1967, he and his poet friends formed the Centre Avenue Poets Theater Workshop, as another expression of black cultural nationalism. In 1968, the *Tulane Drama Review* had a special issue on black theater. "That was the first time I'd seen black plays in print," Wilson said. "There hadn't been any plays on the Negro shelf at the library. So we did them all." Theater could advance political-cultural activism; the vehicle was the Black Horizon Theater, which he started in 1968 with Rob Penny, Sala Udin, and others. Penny would write, Udin would act, and Wilson—the poet—took on the role of director. To learn what that meant, he naturally went to the library, where he found *The Fundamentals of Play Directing* (coincidentally co-written by Lawrence Carra, who taught at nearby Carnegie Mellon University). The new company performed at the A. Leo Weil School in the Hill and also toured, before giving way in the early 1970s to Dr. Vernell Lillie's Kuntu Repertory Theatre, which is still active today.

Moving On, Moving Up

Gradually Wilson began to try his hand at writing plays. In the mid 1970s, his friend Claude Purdy had moved to St. Paul, Minnesota, to work with its black theater company, Penumbra, and he urged Wilson to join him. Just before Wilson's thirty-third birthday, he went, taking with him a satirical play, *Black Bart and the Sacred Hills*, adapted from his poems at Purdy's suggestion. They did a workshop of *Black Bart* in St. Paul, and Wilson stayed. In 1981 he married Judy Oliver, a friend of Purdy's wife.

Wilson once explained that St. Paul and Seattle—cool, northern, Scandinavian cities—appealed to him precisely because of their difference from Pittsburgh, allowing him to look back with more focus and intensity at the true material of August Wilson Country. "It was being in St. Paul, being away from the environment I was most familiar with, that I began hearing the voices," he said. In Pittsburgh, "it was a forest and trees kind of thing." From a distance, he could draw on his memories of the stories, characters, language, and song of the Hill. Moving changed Pittsburgh from a daily adversary to a rich, full resource.

Wilson's own first-staged play was *Recycle*, which drew on the termination of his first marriage. Two other one-act plays from the 1970s are *Homecoming* and *The Coldest Day of the Year*. But he called *Jitney*, written in St. Paul in 1979, his first real play, because in it he dramatized those Pittsburgh memories. "I sat down to write [*Jitney*] and the characters just talked to me. In fact they were talking so fast that I couldn't get it all down." In some ways, *Jitney* is the most Pittsburgh of his Pittsburgh Cycle plays because it arose more directly out of the experiences of his recent life. However, it was not immediately successful. He submitted it twice for workshopping at the prestigious National Playwrights Conference at the Eugene O'Neill Theater Center in Connecticut, but he was turned down. His other unsuccessful submissions to the

O'Neill were *Black Bart and the Sacred Hills, Fullerton Street,* and *Why I Learned to Read.*

In 1982, *Jitney* was staged in Pittsburgh by the small Allegheny Repertory Theatre, the first performance of a Pittsburgh Cycle play, and in 1984 it was staged at St. Paul's Penumbra Theatre. But by then, Wilson had his national breakthrough: his next play, *Ma Rainey's Black Bottom*—a conjunction of a 1976 piece on blues singer Ma Rainey and a separate short play about black musicians—was accepted by the O'Neill for development. Of equal importance, when developing the play at the O'Neill in the summer of 1982, Wilson met its artistic director, Lloyd Richards. Dean of the Yale School of Drama and head of the professional Yale Repertory Theatre, Richards was the director of the break-through Broadway staging twenty-five years earlier of the most influential modern black American play, Lorraine Hansberry's *A Raisin in the Sun.*

It was a turning point in both lives. Richards was the artistic father and collaborator Wilson needed, an experienced director who taught him stagecraft and helped him learn to rewrite. In return, Wilson's plays were a gift to Richards, whose national career was reborn as he went on to direct the first six Wilson plays from workshop to regional theater premieres to Broadway.

From the start, *Ma Rainey* caused a stir. Although plays at the O'Neill are just workshops, not full productions, and are definitely not to be reviewed, Frank Rich, drama critic of the *New York Times,* saw *Ma Rainey* and published an enthusiastic report. Suddenly Wilson was swept up in a frenzy of negotiation, in which some Broadway producers wanted to turn *Ma Rainey* into a musical or hand it over to be altered by more experienced writers. But he held firm, refusing to relinquish control. Eventually, with Richards as director, it premiered at the Yale Repertory Theatre in 1984 and then moved directly to Broadway, where it was clear that a major

December 17, 1999: Constanza Romero and August Wilson during opening festivities at the O'Reilly Theater in downtown Pittsburgh.

new dramatist had suddenly arrived. Wilson was thirty-nine.

Then time sped up, often with one play in initial workshop, another on Broadway, and a third midway from one point to the other, simultaneously. By the time Wilson emerged a Broadway success with *Ma Rainey*, he already had three plays in the Pittsburgh Cycle under way. And when he realized that these first plays were all set in different decades, he conceived his grand design of setting one in each decade of the twentieth century. He was still a newcomer on the national scene, so his plan was greeted with skepticism. But he brought to it the same drive and confidence that had lifted him out of an impoverished childhood.

In 1990, Wilson's second marriage ended and he moved to Seattle. In 1994, he married Constanza Romero, a costume designer whom he had met at Yale—his third marriage, one in each of his three home cities—and they had a daughter, Azula Carmen Wilson, in 1997. Today, Romero serves as the hard-working executor and loving guardian of his artistic legacy.

Pittsburgh, Again

Even as a nonresident, August Wilson remained a good citizen of Pittsburgh, visiting frequently to see his family and friends. But he could be angry, too. On several occasions, notably the 1988 Carnegie Institute "Man and Ideas" series, 1992 University of Pittsburgh Honors Convocation, and 2000 Heinz Lecture Series, Wilson delivered uplifting but accusatory addresses about the black position in both local and national history and culture, talking across the great American racial divide with prophetic force.

He also came to praise the city and its people, as he did at the 1998 "Affirmation of the Blues," a benefit for Community Media at the Carnegie Lecture Hall. Woven out of a love of African American community and art, his talk was shot through with threads of reminiscence over shared early struggles and joys. Honored with him that night were such "elders" as Community Media's Billy Jackson and Kuntu Repertory Theatre founder Dr. Vernell Lillie, who memorialized Wilson when he died as "a brilliant director and poet—a gentle, creative man who loved the arts."

And Wilson came back to Pittsburgh to work. He came for a couple of months in 1996 to revise *Jitney* for its professional rebirth at the Pittsburgh Public Theater. He came again in 1999 to prepare the premiere of *King Hedley II*, which had the honor of opening the Public's new $25-million O'Reilly Theater in the Cultural District.

In 1994, he was here to co-produce the filming of *The Piano Lesson* for television, the only one of his plays so far to make it to the screen. He even came to speak of the beauty of this city that he had not always loved. In 1994, he said, "Like most people, I have this sort of love-hate relationship with Pittsburgh. This is my home and at times I miss it and find it tremendously exciting, and other times I want to catch the first thing out that has wheels."

Spokesman for His Art

Wilson's most popular play, *Fences*, was quickly optioned for film, but he insisted on a black director of his choice, and although he wrote several screenplays of it, as of 2011 the project is still in the offing. But on stage, his clout was great. With his Tony, Olivier Award (London), two Pulitzer Prizes, five New Play Awards or Citations from the American Theatre Critics Association, and seven New York Drama Critics' Circle Awards (an eighth was awarded after he died), he became a centerpiece of contemporary American theater, not just a breakthrough black artist. But he was that, too: in a 1999 roundtable discussion among Wilson and three other black playwrights, Marion McClinton said, "When theaters make money on August Wilson they might say, 'Let's do *two* [black plays] next year.'"

In June 1996, Wilson took on a spokesman role, protesting the marginalization of black theater in a keynote address, "The Ground on Which I Stand," at the annual convention of professional regional theaters. This led to a very public dispute with critic/producer Robert Brustein over the role of race on stage, culminating in their January 1997 public debate in New York City. For a while, theater was back at the center of the national dialogue about race and culture.

Wilson was surprised to be called "rich" in a 2001 *New Yorker* profile by John Lahr, but agreed he was not poor. If you invested one dollar in August Wilson in 1984, when *Ma Rainey* reached Broadway, he said, "You'd have gotten it back and maybe forty cents more." He was generous with his extended family. His awards were many, including more than two dozen honorary doctorates (from the University of Pittsburgh, among others), Rockefeller and Guggenheim fellowships, a National Humanities Medal, and the $250,000 Heinz Award in Arts and Humanities (2003). He was a member of both the American Academy of Arts and Sciences and the American Academy of Arts and Letters.

He was especially proud of receiving the only high school diploma ever issued by the Carnegie Library of Pittsburgh, testimony to the education he gave himself in the stacks of its branches in the Hill and Hazelwood and at the main library in Oakland. That, in turn, is a consequence of (and an ironic commentary on) leaving school when he was accused of falsifying that paper on Napoleon. Wilson's experience of Pittsburgh was always double-edged, providing both nurture and spur, support and challenge, like a sometimes loving, sometimes abusive parent.

Final Year

In an interview in December 2004, Wilson's thoughts turned to mortality. With his sixtieth birthday approaching, he said, "There's more [life] behind me than ahead. I think of dying every day. … At a certain age, you should be prepared to go at any time."

That came quicker than anyone would expect. In June 2005, doctors at Seattle's University of Washington Medical Center discovered that Wilson had a virulent form of liver cancer and recommended an immediate, risky treatment—cancer-fighting drugs injected directly into the tumor—followed by a liver transplant. But the disease proved too far advanced. Wilson said his physicians told him he had a life expectancy of three to five months.

"It's not like poker, you can't throw your hand in," he said in August. "I've lived a blessed life. I'm ready." He added, "I'm glad I finished the cycle." He also noted that when his long-time friend and producer Benjamin Mordecai, the only person to work with him on all ten of his Pittsburgh Cycle plays, had died that spring, the obituary in the *New York Times* included a picture of him and Mordecai together. "That's what gave God this idea," he said. The fierce poignancy of his eulogy for Mordecai in *American Theatre* magazine sounds self-reflexive:

"How do we transform loss? ...Time's healing balm is essentially a hoax. ... Haunted by the specter of my own death, I find solace in Ben's life."

He spent the few months after learning of his illness working on a major rewrite of his final Pittsburgh Cycle play, *Radio Golf*, which had just premiered that April. He was not able to go to Los Angeles for the second production that summer, due to his declining health—the first such absence in his career. He died October 2, 2005, in Seattle.

His funeral service was held in Pittsburgh on October 8 at Soldiers and Sailors Memorial Hall in Oakland, just down the hill from his Hill District. The mourners included many of the now famous actors whom his plays had first brought to national attention. Charles Dutton, who rose to fame as Levee in *Ma Rainey* and Boy Willie in *The Piano Lesson*, read Troy Maxson's speech from *Fences*: "Death ain't nothing but a fastball on the outside corner. And you know what I'll do to that! ... You can kiss it good-bye. ... That's all death is to me." Afterward, the funeral cortege wound circuitously back through the Hill, where the streets were alive with people paying final respect to one of its most famous sons, before heading north to Greenwood Cemetery in O'Hara Township, where he was buried near the graves of many from the Hill, including those of his mother and grandmother.

Legacy

Since Wilson's death, Pittsburgh has debated how to honor his life and work. One honor is the $42-million August Wilson Center for African American Culture, which opened in 2009, downtown on Liberty Avenue. On May 30, 2007, a state historical marker was placed at his boyhood home at 1727 Bedford Avenue, now owned by his nephew, Paul A. Ellis, Jr. After much delay, on February 26, 2008, Pittsburgh City Council designated the building as a City Historic Structure.

In November 2010, the Daisy Wilson Artist Community, Inc., a nonprofit named in honor of Wilson's mother, announced plans to restore 1727 Bedford Avenue and "develop the site to house a world-class artist-in-residence program."

But Wilson's Pittsburgh legacy is not mainly bricks and mortar. In addition to its professional premieres of *Jitney* and *King Hedley II*, the Pittsburgh Public Theater has produced all of Wilson's other Pittsburgh Cycle plays (see summaries—page 121) as soon as rights were available. Many have been staged by the Kuntu Repertory Theatre, with which he was active in the 1970s, and by Pittsburgh Playwrights Theatre, which in 2004 began staging all ten plays in the order of their Broadway premieres, one each year.

Nationally, many of the major regional theaters are continuing their journey through the plays, while others return to them for revivals. Wilson's plays opened new avenues for black artists and, by changing the way theater approaches race, changed the business of theater, too.

The speed with which the plays established themselves as essential fare not only demonstrates their felt quality and widespread appeal, but also suggests they may answer a deep need. That certainly includes what they most obviously offer—a passionate yet accessible dramatization of the black experience. The ongoing tragedy of the great African Diaspora is a theme of epic scope. The plays' subtlety and depth of anger, expressed with cunning, linguistic richness, and raw power in their plots but also in the many tales their characters tell, keep them surprising, vigorous, and true.

At regional theaters and on Broadway, Wilson's audiences have been predominantly white. Clearly he offers something a white audience wants to experience. It is not just that *Ma Rainey* speaks to anyone who has suffered economic exploitation, that *Fences* awakens memories of many family battles, or that we all share the terrors of separation and loss dramatized in *Joe Turner*. Though Wilson strikes these deep,

August Wilson and Christopher Rawson at the Kennedy Center, November 13, 1991. Rawson presented Wilson with the Best Play Award of the American Theatre Critics Association for *Two Trains Running*.

perhaps universal chords, he gives life to particular times and places. Audiences can also trust the plays as vivid fictions, not just as sociology or polemic.

Perhaps white audiences respond to Wilson as the classic truth-teller who comes from another place. "Blacks know more about whites in white culture and white life than whites know about blacks. We have to know because our survival depends on it," he told Bill Moyers. White characters make few appearances in Wilson's plays (just five characters out of seventy-seven), but white society is all around, pressing in. A white audience sees itself anew through the anger, humor, frustration, and perspective of Wilson's black characters, while black audiences experience much that they have often known but have never seen so pungently and publicly expressed.

In his funeral eulogy, Marion McClinton, director of *Jitney* and *King Hedley II*, the two Wilson plays that premiered in Pittsburgh, said that "August Wilson changed the lives of young men and women, of old men and women, [and] of men and women in between, black, white, red, yellow." Wilson, he said, "loved his people and he would not let them not love themselves." □

When I was twenty, I left the library and I left my mother's house and went out into the community of the Hill District to learn what it was they had to teach me. I went out on the street corners, the bars and restaurants and barbershops to learn how to be a man, to learn what codes of conduct the community sanctioned and how I might best live a full and dedicated life. What did the community of people among whom I lived and shared a common past expect of me?

I moved from Pittsburgh to St. Paul, Minnesota, on March 5, 1978. I left Pittsburgh but Pittsburgh never left me. It was on these streets in this community in this city that I came into manhood and I have a fierce affection for the Hill District and the people who raised me, who have sanctioned my life and ultimately provide it with its meaning.

AUGUST WILSON, "FEED YOUR MIND, THE REST WILL FOLLOW,"
PITTSBURGH POST-GAZETTE, MARCH 28, 1999:
ON THE OCCASION OF THE 100TH ANNIVERSARY OF THE
CARNEGIE LIBRARY OF PITTSBURGH'S HILL DISTRICT BRANCH

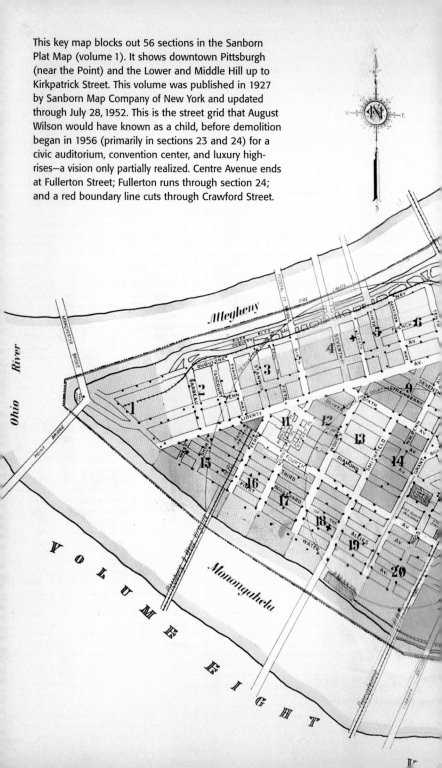

This key map blocks out 56 sections in the Sanborn Plat Map (volume 1). It shows downtown Pittsburgh (near the Point) and the Lower and Middle Hill up to Kirkpatrick Street. This volume was published in 1927 by Sanborn Map Company of New York and updated through July 28, 1952. This is the street grid that August Wilson would have known as a child, before demolition began in 1956 (primarily in sections 23 and 24) for a civic auditorium, convention center, and luxury high-rises—a vision only partially realized. Centre Avenue ends at Fullerton Street; Fullerton runs through section 24; and a red boundary line cuts through Crawford Street.

1956: The Civic Arena and new street grid are superimposed on a view of the Lower Hill, with downtown Pittsburgh beyond. The new Centre Avenue (mid-photo) is to extend through the Lower Hill, and it curves as it approaches downtown. August Wilson was about ten years old when redevelopment began. In 1958, his mother moved the family to Hazelwood.

It is August in Pittsburgh, 1911. The sun falls out of heaven like a stone. The fires of the steel mill rage with a combined sense of industry and progress. Barges loaded with coal and iron ore trudge up the river to the mill towns that dot the Monongahela and return with fresh, hard, gleaming steel. The city flexes its muscles. Men throw countless bridges across the rivers, lay roads and carve tunnels through the hills sprouting with houses.

AUGUST WILSON, INTRODUCTION TO
JOE TURNER'S COME AND GONE

The Hill and the African American Experience

Laurence A. Glasco

The Hill District is perhaps Pittsburgh's best situated neighborhood, sloping upward all the way from downtown to Bigelow Boulevard in Oakland, giving it magnificent panoramas to the west, north, and south. It also is the city's most storied and historic neighborhood, whose trees and pastures and woods made it attractive for the city's elite, who began moving there in the 1820s to escape downtown congestion and grime. It subsequently became the principal destination of new immigrants, beginning with Irish and Germans in the 1850s and then, around the turn of the twentieth century, continuing with Southern and Eastern European immigrants, especially Jews and Italians.

Ethnic Diversity

Blacks were among the neighborhood's original settlers, but job discrimination kept their numbers small until the 1880s. Then, Pittsburgh's booming economy created so many job opportunities—notably in hauling and carting, day labor, and personal service—that blacks increasingly were attracted to the city. They settled mainly in the Hill. The black presence in the Hill continued to increase when World War I cut off European immigration and created a labor shortage so severe that steel and other industries changed their hiring policies and began employing blacks.

Between 1910 and 1930, the resulting migratory wave boosted Pittsburgh's black population from 25,000 to over 50,000. As whites began moving out of the Hill, the black presence increased until the Hill became majority black around 1930. The 1940s census still listed twenty-five

Louis and Bella Siger, in a photo from the 1940s, in Bella's Market at 1727 Bedford Avenue. In 1949, four years after her husband's death, Bella purchased the building and continued to operate the market through 1965. August Wilson lived with his mother and siblings in the rear apartment of the building.

nationalities in the Hill. They typically lived in their own racial and ethnic clusters: Jews concentrated in the southern part of the Hill between Wylie and Fifth avenues; Italians lived north of Wylie Avenue around lower Webster and Bedford avenues; and Syrians, Armenians, Lebanese, and Greeks clustered around the Italians on lower Bedford and Webster avenues. The Irish settled around Tunnel and Congress streets and on Webster and Fifth avenues.

There was considerable ethnic and racial overlap in housing. In 1920, one-third of blacks in the Hill lived within five doors of a white neighbor—typically Jewish. Children attended integrated schools together because Pittsburgh had desegregated in the 1870s. Thelma Lovette, a black resident born and raised in the Hill, recalls shopping in the 1930s with people of different backgrounds along Logan Street, buying groceries, poultry, and dry goods at Jewish and Italian shops, while conversing with friends and neighbors. Johnny Butera, of Italian descent, lived at 1725 Bedford Avenue. Louis and Beatrice (Bella) Siger, a Jewish family, operated Bella's Market in the storefront of 1727 Bedford Avenue, Wilson's childhood home. Up and down the street lived Syrians, Greeks, Italians, and blacks. Butera recalled that neighbors seldom socialized across racial lines, but were friendly with one another and could be counted on in a pinch.

Cultural Vitality

Wylie Avenue constituted the heart of the Hill's business district for blacks, but black merchants operated alongside whites on Centre Avenue as well. Lillian Allen, a leading black beautician of the Hill, recalled the community during an interview in 2004, at age ninety-six:

> The Hill was an entity of its own. At one time it boasted five movie theaters. … On Sundays, there was a line waiting to eat at [Nesbit's] or take home Nesbit's delicious pies.

Gordon's Shoes was on the southeast corner of Centre Avenue and Kirpatrick Street in the Hill. This photograph by *Pittsburgh Courier's* Teenie Harris, c. 1938–50, was taken from the Gulf service station on the northwest corner, where the Carnegie Library of Pittsburgh's Hill District branch is now. Dom Magasano owned the Gulf station from 1947 to 1961; then he sold it to Herb Bean.

Around the corner on Centre Avenue was the plant of Robert L. Vann's Pittsburgh Courier, *our weekly newspaper. … Also on Centre Avenue was the Elmore Theater. … Back then the Hill was very proud of the New Granada and Roosevelt theaters, where uniformed ushers seated you, like downtown. … On Fullerton Street was The Rhumba that showed old movies. … The building had a nightclub in the basement called The Bambola. The club was the haunt of the nightlife people. … The Halloween night party at The Bambola was a time when the lesbians and the gays could come out of the closet. … Among the popular places to go was William Stanley's bar on Fullerton and Wylie … [T]he Crawford Grill [was] a*

place to relax over a drink and enjoy good food and jazz.
… Fireman's Department Store on Centre Avenue filled
the needs of the average family and Gordon's Shoes fitted
the feet of all sizes and types. Johnson's Studios and Lee's
Florist were represented at most weddings, funerals,
and banquets.

From the 1920s on, blacks and whites flocked to the bars and night spots in the Hill that attracted some of the nation's finest jazz musicians. Marie's and Lola's, small and stuffy clubs, provided spots for late-night jam sessions, and helped make Pittsburgh a center for nurturing internationally known musicians. Jazz notables born, reared, or nurtured in Pittsburgh included Billy Strayhorn, Kenny Clarke, Art Blakey, Earl ("Fatha") Hines, Roy Eldridge, and Leroy Brown, in addition to such notable female musicians as Lena Horne, Mary Lou Williams, Louise Mann, and Maxine Sullivan. Mary Dee, a popular disk jockey in the 1950s, labeled the intersection of Wylie Avenue and Fullerton Street as the "Crossroads of the World."

The cultural life of the Hill—and the social, political, and economic life of black Pittsburgh—filled the pages of the *Pittsburgh Courier*, one of the community's outstanding achievements. Edited by Robert L. Vann, the *Courier* fostered a sense of community and promoted black interests in the city. The paper's four editions—local, Northern, Eastern, and Southern—were distributed in all forty-eight states plus Europe, Africa, Canada, the Philippines, and the West Indies. In 1938, its circulation reached 250,000, making it the largest all-black weekly in the world. Ultimately, the *Courier* grew to fourteen editions, with a peak circulation of 357,212 in 1942. Ironically, as white papers included more news about blacks, the circulation of the *Courier* dropped until it was bought by Chicago interests in 1966, and then rejuvenated and renamed the *New Pittsburgh Courier*.

Housing

A major problem in the 1940s and 1950s was housing. Despite holding jobs, blacks could not find decent housing. The situation was especially acute in the Hill, which had the city's oldest and most deteriorated housing stock. About the only new housing in the Hill were two massive public housing projects, Bedford Dwellings, located on the northern part of the Hill just off Bedford Avenue, and the Terrace Village complex in the southern part of the Hill, ultimately stretching all the way to Oakland. Terrace Village was one of the nation's earliest and largest housing projects, and, in October 1940, President Franklin Roosevelt came to Pittsburgh to open the first part of it. The projects were racially integrated, had grassy courtyards where kids could play, boasted modern kitchens, and had strict rules of behavior and maintenance. They were the envy of many working-class whites and blacks living in dilapidated dwellings without toilets and running water.

However, progress in residential integration proved difficult. As early as 1952 the city had passed a fair-housing ordinance that helped some blacks find homes in formerly all-white neighborhoods. But such neighborhoods, once integrated, typically became majority black. Pittsburgh, like other cities, remained highly segregated, with a segregation index in the high seventies, meaning that over seventy percent of blacks in highly concentrated black neighborhoods would have to move to "white" neighborhoods to achieve an index of zero, or total integration.

Public housing became increasingly segregated and neglected, despite efforts by activists such as Bishop Charles Foggie of Wesley Center A.M.E. Zion Church, who worked valiantly to improve conditions.

Opposite: A view from Soho in May 1951, looking up hill from Forbes Avenue. Older housing contrasts with the new Terrace Village.

FORBES COFFEE SH

These photos show construction in 1955 of the Penn-Lincoln Parkway (above) and in 1956 of the Boulevard of the Allies eastbound ramp leading to the Parkway (opposite). The highways are just below the Hill District. Notice the Brady Street Bridge (above left) over the Monongahela River and the Jones & Laughlin steel mill (opposite)— places mentioned in five of August Wilson's plays: *Gem of the Ocean*, *Joe Turner's Come and Gone*, *Fences*, *Two Trains Running*, and *Jitney*. The Brady Street Bridge was demolished in 1978, the year Wilson left Pittsburgh for St. Paul, Minnesota. (The Birmingham Bridge replaced it.)

The J&L/LTV steel mill (above right) was within walking distance of the Hill District; it closed in 1988.

Wilson grew up in Pittsburgh during a time of great change. During Pittsburgh's Renaissance, from the mid 1940s to early 1970s, smoke-control and water-purification laws were enforced and massive clearances eventually resulted in the creation of Point State Park and in the redevelopment (unsuccessfully) of portions of the Hill District, North Side, and East Liberty.

Urban Renewal

In 1956, as part of an effort to create a cultural district on the edge of downtown, the city reduced the Lower Hill to rubble, eliminating over 400 businesses and displacing some 8,000 residents, most of whom were black. In its place was erected a mammoth, technologically advanced civic auditorium (completed in 1961) for light opera, concerts, and athletic events, plus one apartment building far too expensive for residents of the area.

The plan stemmed from a relatively new concept called "urban renewal" and was implemented by a new city agency, the Urban Redevelopment Authority (URA). The hope was to change Pittsburgh's "Smoky City" image and stop the out-migration of its middle class. The city gained an arena (the Civic Arena, later Mellon Arena), surface parking, and Washington Plaza Apartments (designed by I. M. Pei in 1958 and opened in 1964), but lost the social, economic, cultural, and emotional center of its most historic neighborhood.

At first many blacks had faith in the proposed redevelopment of the Lower Hill. The *Pittsburgh Courier* supported it, as did the community's leading political figures, Homer S. Brown and Paul Jones. To understand why, one must note that the Hill was not monolithic. The Lower Hill, affectionately termed "Pot Likker Flats" by *Courier* editor Frank E. Bolden, had jazz spots of note, but also bars, brothels, and rooming houses of notoriety. It had some stable and hard-working families, but also many drifters, gamblers, prostitutes, and pimps. And its housing, streets, and sanitary conditions were, for the most part, reprehensible. This area between downtown and Crawford Street was what black leadership wanted to see redeveloped, and that in fact was what got torn down. Black leaders were not thinking of redeveloping the area between Crawford Street and Herron Avenue, known as the Middle Hill, which had a higher proportion of homeowners. And certainly they were not thinking of the Upper Hill, located

C. 1961: A view of the Lower Hill from the Monongahela River, with the once-flourishing commercial neighborhood destroyed, the Civic Arena nearing completion, and Centre Avenue extended downtown.

east of Herron Avenue, called "Sugar Top" by many and "Scotch-and-Soda-Highlands" by Bolden, where much of the black middle and upper classes lived more comfortably.

Redevelopment turned into a disaster. The city promised that those evicted would get new housing, which many understood to mean more units like the well-regarded public housing projects. Promised housing did not materialize, however, and evicted residents scrambled to find places to live in other neighborhoods, mainly the Middle Hill and Homewood, bringing overcrowding and tension to those areas.

The city planned to extend redevelopment deeper into the Hill, well beyond Crawford Street. When this became clear, the black community organized and stopped it. In 1968, James McCoy, Jr., a civil rights officer from the United Steelworkers who created the United Negro Protest Committee (UNPC) in 1963, and Frankie Pace, a highly respected business woman and music teacher, spearheaded a grassroots mobilization of residents. They rented space on a billboard proclaiming "NO Redevelopment Beyond This Point" at the corner of Centre Avenue and Crawford Street, across from St. Benedict the Moor Church.

Churches

Churches represented a positive response to the social and emotional needs of the immigrants and migrants in particular. They helped create a "moral community" in the midst of the temptations of the secular city. Their services reinforced an intense religiosity and relieved the many frustrations of adjusting to urban life.

Although class differences persisted among black congregations, established churches responded to calls for racial unity during the civil rights movement. This involvement of churches in direct political activity was new to the black community, and helped middle-class churches reach out to help their poorer brothers.

OLD JOE: **You trying to tear down my house is chaos. It ain't harmony. If we had harmony you'd be helping me paint it.**

RADIO GOLF: ACT ONE, SCENE 4

BECKER: **… I say we stay here. We already here. The people know we here. We been here for eighteen years … and I don't see no reason to move. City or no city. I look around and all I see is boarded-up buildings. Some of them been boarded up for more than ten years. If they want to build some houses that's when they can tear it down. When they ready to build the houses. They board this place up the first of the month and let it sit boarded up for the next fifteen … twenty years.**

JITNEY: ACT TWO, SCENE 2

Civil Rights and Black Consciousness

Civil rights demonstrations dominated the 1960s. Alma Speed Fox, long active in the National Association for the Advancement of Colored People (NAACP), says it seemed "there was some picket line to get on every single solitary week." The NAACP, under the leadership of Byrd Brown, organized marches and picketing for equal opportunity directed against many institutions during the 1960s, including Duquesne Light, Mine Safety Appliances, Sears Roebuck, Kaufmann's, Horne's, and Gimbels department stores, the Board of Education, and the University of Pittsburgh.

Women's groups also provided support for civil rights issues. This was especially true of the YWCA, under the inter-racial leadership of Frieda Shapira (wife of a founder of Giant Eagle grocery), Lavera Brown, and Jan Neffke. Thelma Lovette provided support, both direct and indirect, in marches and in behind-the-scenes organizational work through involvement with many civic organizations, from the Girls Scouts, Block Clubs, and YMCA to the Urban League and NAACP.

The Southern civil rights movement inspired local activism. Sam Howze, for example, after growing up in the Lower Hill and the Bedford Dwellings housing project, went to fight segregation in Mississippi, where he was radicalized by arrests and beatings. In 1968, after returning to Pittsburgh, he changed his name to Sala Udin and joined August Wilson and Rob Penny in creating Black Horizon Theater, a black-consciousness theater group. The next year he and his friend, Jake Milliones, founded Ile Elegba, a drug treatment program in the Hill. In 1992, Udin joined Milliones, then Councilman, in working to change Pittsburgh politics. After Milliones's death in 1993, Udin became spokesman for his Hill District constituents on City Council in 1995.

Whites also participated in the civil rights struggle. Gail Falk (daughter of Dr. Leslie Falk, and not related to the Falks of the medical fund) traveled to Mississippi with Hill District resident Robert M. Lavelle and Northside resident Sharry Everett. Philip B. Hallen, president of the Maurice Falk Medical Fund, drove truckloads of medicine to volunteers in Mississippi. The Thomas Merton Center sent volunteers South. Father Donald McIlvane, a Roman Catholic priest active on the Race and Religion Council, marched in Selma, Alabama. And the indefatigable Marguerite Hofer recruited more than a dozen Presbyterian ministers to volunteer for service in the South. More than eight of those ministers went to Mississippi, and nearly all were arrested there. These campaigns by Pittsburghers, black and white, secular and churched, moderate and militant, were part of a national effort that, in 1964 and 1965, helped pass the Civil Rights and Voting Rights Acts, the most important civil rights legislation since Reconstruction.

A major manifestation of new black pride and unity occurred in March 1968 at the Hill District's New Granada Theater during a three-day observance of the death of Malcolm X, organized by Sala Udin and the militant Afro-American Institute. "When you see a revolution going on—and it's your revolution—you don't get out of the way—you join it," advised August Wilson, who was in attendance. Wilson's mentor and co-writer, Rob Penny, urged inner as well as outer blackness: "Wash yo' hair, cleanse yo' mind, dig yo' self, an' come on home." Curtiss Porter, who was a faculty member at the University of Pittsburgh, reveled in the presence of "young and old, poor and kinda' rich, high class and low down, militant and middle class, straight hair and straightened hair, wigs and natural naps—every spectrum of black Pittsburgh was represented."

Blue-Collar Struggles

Blue-collar employment proved the most difficult and explosive of all issues. When the decline of the steel industry accelerated after World War II, even a liberal union like the United Steel Workers had difficulty ending practices by which blacks held the least desirable jobs. Despite the efforts of James McCoy, Jr., and his United Negro Protest Committee, little changed even after lawsuits and federal pressure forced the steel companies and the steelworkers' union to sign a Consent Decree in 1974, paying damages to black workers and allowing them to transfer seniority from their previous jobs. The Decree generated fierce resentment among white workers, and its long-run effects were minimal.

If the problem in the steel industry was getting promoted, the problem in the building trades was getting hired. With few exceptions, the trades were determined to remain as lily-white as possible. Organized efforts to change this began with the Negro American Labor Council (NALC), a national coalition of black industrial unionists led by A. Philip Randolph. In 1961, the NALC and the NAACP staged mass picketing of the Civic Arena, where only eight blacks out of a workforce of several hundred were being employed.

Exceptionally good leadership allowed at least one employment victory. In 1967, Nate Smith, the only black member of the Operating Engineers' Union, formed "Operation Dig" and persuaded his union to accept some ninety blacks whom he had trained. Smith's success with Operation Dig and the Operating Engineers, unfortunately, was not duplicated with other building trades. In 1969, therefore, impelled by the anger and militancy that followed the riots of 1968, Operation Dig, the Bidwell Training Center, the NAACP, and a number of other community and anti-poverty organizations formed the Black Construction Coalition (BCC). This group, of which Clyde Jackson was a prime mover, halted work on ten building projects, put 800 marchers on the Northside and, after two weeks of demonstrations, brought the city to the brink of massive violence. Reverend Jimmy Joe Robinson of Bidwell Presbyterian Church in Manchester was active throughout the demonstrations, and Robinson and NAACP President Byrd Brown suffered beatings and macing during one particularly violent police confrontation on the Manchester Bridge. Their efforts produced the Pittsburgh Plan (1969), hailed as a national model to train blacks for construction jobs, but over-demanding activists and recalcitrant unions undermined the agreement.

In the context of a collapsing industrial base and systematic job discrimination, government efforts such as President Lyndon Johnson's 1964 "War on Poverty" embodied laudable intentions but could make only marginal improvements. The Economic Opportunity Act, created to turn President Johnson's dream into a reality, initiated a whole raft of anti-poverty agencies, including Job Corps, VISTA, Community Action Programs, Model Cities, Head Start, Legal Services, Foster Grandparents, and the Office of Economic Opportunity.

Pittsburgh's principal anti-poverty agency, the Mayor's Committee on Human Resources (later Community Action Pittsburgh—CAP), headed by David Epperson, won praise from the local press and was cited by the federal government as a model, but had no more success than others around the country. One study concluded that the committee's ineffective-ness stemmed partly from the geographic dispersal of its clients and partly from a surfeit of competing agencies, such as Model Cities. Together, such competing leaders and priorities deprived local blacks of the unity needed to force the bureau-cracy to respond. However, CAP left a legacy of institutions, including the Alma Illery Health Center, the community development corporations, and Head Start.

In the end, blacks in the blue-collar civil rights struggle had little to show for their efforts. As frustration increased, individual militants entered the battle. William "Bouie" Haden, a self-appointed leader with a long history of police involve-ment and an intimidating demeanor and appearance, led a small but noisy demonstration in 1967 that forced the

Homewood Giant Eagle to appoint a black manager to its Frankstown store. But even such individual acts of militancy could do little to change the deep structural problems that frustrated so many blacks, especially the young.

White-Collar Gains

Civil rights gains benefited white-collar blacks much more than blue-collar blacks. Hiring for white-collar positions was aided by the fact that America's economy, and Pittsburgh's in particular, was shifting from an industrial to a service base. Shortly after World War II, St. Francis and Montefiore hospitals began admitting blacks to their nursing schools, and Montefiore granted staff privileges to Dr. James Lewis, a dentist, and visiting privileges to Dr. Charles Burks, a physician. Shortly afterwards, St. Francis hired Dr. Earl Belle Smith, a noted black surgeon.

In 1947, Urban League staffer K. Leroy Irvis opened up clerical positions by organizing pickets of downtown department stores. And in the 1950s, Arthur J. Edmunds of the Urban League and Fletcher Byrom of Koppers were successful in persuading local corporations to hire additional blacks in white-collar positions.

A demonstration against Duquesne Light in the early 1960s provided a breakthrough in white-collar and, to a lesser extent, blue-collar, hiring. This successful assault unfolded after Byrd Brown, president of the NAACP, sensing the need for total community involvement in an organization still perceived as somewhat elitist, formed the Labor and Industry Committee under the leadership of James McCoy, Jr. He and his UNPC turned out some 5,000 pickets, the largest civil rights demonstration in Pittsburgh up to that time; they shocked the business community. The success against Duquesne Light caused other employers to capitulate soon after they were targeted, including Union Switch and Signal in East Liberty,

Penn Sheraton Hotel, and Horne's department store downtown. One participant, Douglas King, recalls that businesses began telephoning the NAACP, pro-actively promising to hire blacks.

Education

White-collar and professional gains for blacks in Pittsburgh were noteworthy in the field of education. The Board of Education hired its first black teacher, Lawrence Peeler, in 1937, but made only token hires until the 1950s and 1960s. In 1968, blacks organized a take-over of the computer center at the University of Pittsburgh that resulted in the establishment of a Black Studies Department, followed by programs to increase the number of black faculty, staff, and students. Jack Daniel became the first chairman of the Black Action Society.

If blacks made gains in the late 1960s as teachers, the same could not be said for their situation as pupils. The public school system failed to educate black students. The challenge for public education remained neighborhood-based segregation and academic underperformance. Many black leaders, including Reverend Elmer Williams and Jake Milliones and his wife Margaret, focused on issues of integration and quality education, recognizing these as key to future advancement. But meaningful integration was never achieved, even with promising experiments such as magnet schools, with specialized academic interests. Nor was the black-white performance gap substantially reduced, although the potential for doing so was demonstrated by principals Doris Brevard, Janet Bell, Vivian Williams, and Louis Venson, whose pupils at Vann, Westwood, Madison, and Beltzhoover consistently exceeded national norms in reading and mathematics.

Riots of 1968

Given the grim situation in housing, employment, and education, it is remarkable that Pittsburgh escaped the "Long Hot

Summer" riots that broke out in major cities in the mid-1960s. However, in a prescient series of articles that appeared in the *New Pittsburgh Courier* in March 1968, Carl Morris noted that militants in Pittsburgh had seen other cities' riots on television and were rumored to be planning a "B-Day," or "Burn Day," for May 1968.

With the assassination of Martin Luther King, Jr., in Memphis, Tennessee, on April 4, 1968, Morris' warning came true a bit early, and Pittsburgh joined other cities in spontaneous, convulsive riots. King was assassinated on a Thursday, and riots in Pittsburgh started on Friday and continued through Sunday. Remarkably, Pittsburgh suffered only one death, a white woman who was killed by firebombers in Homewood. The difference in Pittsburgh was partly due to the decision of Mayor Joseph Barr to informally delegate responsibility for calming things in the Hill to K. Leroy Irvis, the Hill District's respected state representative who lived and had his office near Centre Avenue and Kirkpatrick Street, the epicenter of the violence. On the Northside, Reverend Jimmy Joe Robinson and Irvis worked together to dissuade armed and angry young men from escalating the violence.

Irvis and Robinson helped save lives, but could not stop the property damage, especially in the Hill, whose business corridor along Centre Avenue was devastated. Over 500 fires destroyed much of the business district and drove many merchants out of business and out of the Hill. Ironically, the riots completed the destruction that urban renewal had begun.

Post-Riot Black Pittsburgh

The assassination of King and the riots of 1968 marked the end of the civil rights movement, at least of its integrated, non-violent phase. The new laws had made little difference in the daily lives of poor blacks.

The racial isolation of the black community increased as whites continued to leave for the suburbs. The inner cities became more segregated, which made issues of housing, employment, and education less amenable to civil rights tactics and coalitions that had worked in the past. As the interracial alliance began to unravel, blacks increasingly felt a need to do for themselves.

The urge to "do for self"—a mantra of the Nation of Islam made most popular by Malcolm X at the time—did not necessarily reflect bitterness. For some it was the natural expression of independence and self-confidence. In the 1950s, for example, Silas Knox had started the Owl Cab company, an independent black-owned taxi service. Robert R. Lavelle founded a real estate business to increase home ownership among Hill District residents and other blacks. Then, Mr. Lavelle revived the Dwelling House Savings and Loan Association so blacks would have a source for mortgage loans and an alternative to lenders who redlined black neighborhoods and discriminated against black borrowers. Herb Bean owned several gas stations in the 1960s, notably one at the corner of Centre Avenue and Kirkpatrick Street, in the heart of the Hill. William Pryor, a master furrier operating in the Hill District since 1947, donated time and money to all sorts of community causes. Clyde Jackson established Wylie-Centre Industry, the world's first black-owned nail factory. Milton Washington's Allegheny Housing Rehabilitation Corporation became deeply involved in developing, managing, and rehabbing moderate- and low-income housing throughout the city and region.

Even after the riots and the rise of attitudes of separatism and "black power," committed whites continued to work for black community development. Philip B. Hallen remained in the struggle, working with James McCoy, Jr., who had established Freedom House Enterprises, and Dr. Peter Safar of the University of Pittsburgh's medical school, to establish the Freedom House ambulance program, located on Centre Avenue near Devilliers Street. Meant to provide on-the-spot treatment and transportation to hospitals for Hill District

TROY: … This is my house. Bought and paid for. In full. Took me fifteen years. And if you wanna go in my house and I'm sitting on the steps … you say excuse me. Like your mama taught you.

Fences: Act Two, Scene 4

HARMOND: When I called the union and tried to get you on the job they said you weren't a member.

STERLING: Naw … you don't understand. I'm my own union. I got my own everything. Except my own bank. But I got my own truck. I got my own tools. I got my own rules and I got my own union.

Radio Golf: Act One, Scene 4

blacks whom police ambulances shunned, the service pioneered innovative techniques and became the national model upon which pre-hospital emergency care is now based. Its success, ironically, led to its demise when Pittsburgh folded it into a new, largely white-operated, Emergency Medical System (EMS).

Nonetheless, in Pittsburgh as in the rest of the nation, while Robert R. Lavelle and Clyde Jackson and Milton Washington spoke of "empowerment," others spoke of "black power" and questioned the goal of racial integration. This "black mood," as Carl Morris termed it in 1968, dominated the nation and Pittsburgh for the next quarter century as battles over community control, affirmative action, busing, Louis Farrakhan, and Jesse Jackson gripped the land, and issues of drugs, crime, and family break-up consumed blacks' attention. The mood turned sour among many in white America as well, and accelerated in the 1980s as Republicans won the votes of angry, fearful whites by using Willie Horton, the black rapist-murderer, to personify black men, and so-called "Welfare Queens" to personify black women.

The 1990s, the last decade of Wilson's Pittsburgh Cycle, offered a glimmer of hope for black Pittsburgh and the Hill. Hope was made manifest in many areas of black life. It could be seen in a labor market so tight that black unemployment dropped by more than half and the overall rate of serious crime in the city fell substantially. It could be seen in the decline, from 74 to 67, in the index of segregation, the first decline in living memory. It could be seen physically in the construction of Williams Square, a black-owned office building on Centre Avenue. It could be seen in the ongoing conversions of public housing into mixed-income neighborhoods of attractive townhouses in the Hill and Oakland. And it could be seen in the different way in which this process of conversion had been handled, with involvement of local residents and the inclusion of substantial numbers of former public housing residents in the new developments.

August Wilson's cycle ends in the 1990s with *Radio Golf* depicting the efforts of a well-meaning black realtor to redevelop the Hill until he realizes that redevelopment could wipe out its rich history. Whether Wilson was thinking of the 1950s or the 1990s, the latter decade saw, in fact, the Urban Redevelopment Authority of Pittsburgh fund construction in the Lower Hill of Crawford Square town homes and apartments (see page 65). Their impact led a local newspaper to speak of them as part of the "Rebirth of the Hill."

Redevelopment continues. New housing, such as The Legacy apartments, continues to be built, and Bedford Dwellings and Terrace Village have been largely converted into townhouses and mixed-income residences. A new Carnegie branch library has been constructed at 2177 Centre Avenue, and Duquesne University's Mylan School of Pharmacy has opened a pharmacy in the Triangle Shops Plaza on Centre Avenue.

Construction is progressing in 2011 on a new YMCA, named in honor of Thelma Lovette. A grocery store is finally to open in The Hill. The Crawford Grill has been purchased by investors who hope to restore the historic landmark. The New Granada Theater, vacant since the mid-1970s and an icon of the neighborhood's storied past, has been stabilized and is the object of intense revitalization efforts. August Wilson's family now owns the empty building at 1727 Bedford Avenue, where the playwright grew up, and is seeking to preserve and develop the historic structure.

There are other sites, too, with their own histories, providing connections between the Hill District's past and future. Together, they recall black Pittsburgh's rich history. They remind us that the Hill remains a dynamic, ever-changing place whose residents care about and shape its future. □

The Legacy apartments for seniors, designed by Rothschild Doyno Collaborative, opened in 2007. Its Wylie Avenue façade is inscribed with the names of people who are part of the Hill's jazz history: Walt Harper, Roger Humphries, Stanley Turrentine, George Benson, Ahmad Jamal, Art Blakey, Billy Eckstine, Earl "Fatha" Hines, Erroll Garner, Mary Lou Williams, Gus Greenlee, and Mary Dee. Pat's Place was located at the far end of The Legacy, on the southwest corner of Wylie at Elmore Street.

I stood around in Pat's Place and listened to [the elders of the community]. They talked philosophy, history; they discussed whatever the topic of the day was—the newspapers, the politics of the city, the baseball games, and invariably they would talk about themselves and their lives when they were young men. And so a lot of what I know of the history of blacks in a very personal sense I picked up standing there in Pat's Place.

CONVERSATIONS WITH AUGUST WILSON:
"AUGUST WILSON: AN INTERVIEW," VERA SHEPPARD, 1990

As 2010 came to a close, the Lower Hill was again the site of controversy and proposed change. The board of the Sports & Exhibition Authority of Pittsburgh and Allegheny County voted unanimously on September 16, 2010, to demolish the Civic Arena, in order to clear the way for a mixed-use development proposed by the Pittsburgh Penguins that would reestablish an urban street grid. However, on November 24, a Hill District resident nominated the vacant structure as a City of Pittsburgh Historic Structure, thus setting a review process in motion.

BLACK MARY: This house is sanctuary!
It's been sanctuary for a long time.
You know that. Everybody know that.
This is 1839 Wylie Avenue.

GEM OF THE OCEAN: ACT TWO, SCENE 4

STERLING: ... I left out of there and was
walking by Aunt Ester's. I saw the
light on and I figure she might be up,
so I stopped to see her. They led me
into the hallway and then through
some curtains into this room ... and
she was just sitting there. I talked to
her a long while. Told her my whole
life story.

TWO TRAINS RUNNING: ACT TWO, SCENE 4

Guide

Hill District Tour

Tour of Sites Beyond the Hill

The tour content is based on writings by and interviews with August Wilson, the plays themselves, and historical research by the authors and editors.

Hill District Map

1. Freedom Corner Monument
2. St. Benedict the Moor Church
3. Crawford Street (rented room; demolished)
4. Connelley Trade School
5. Letsche Education Center
6. St. George Syrian/Antiochian Orthodox Church
7. 1621 Bedford Avenue
8. 1710 Bedford Avenue
9. 1712 Bedford Avenue
10. 1725 Bedford Avenue
11. 1727 Bedford Avenue
12. 1600 Block Webster Avenue/Manilla Street
13. Loendi Club (demolished)
14. Arcena Street View
15. Miller African Centered Academy
16. Aunt Ester's House (imagined)
17. The First Muslim Mosque of Pittsburgh
18. Westbrook Jitney Station
19. Crawford Grill No. 2
20. Eddie's Restaurant (demolished)
21. West Funeral Home
22. Tuberculosis League Hospital Historic District
23. St. Benedict the Moor School
24. Pittsburgh Weil School
25. Lutz's Meat Market
26. Ellis Hotel (demolished)
27. Halfway Art Gallery (demolished)
28. Hill Community Development Corporation
29. New Granada Theater
30. Workingmen's Civic Club (demolished)
31. Hill House Association
32. Kaufmann Auditorium

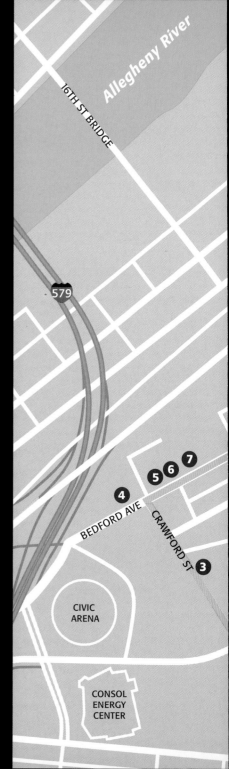

Hill District Tour

General Notes

1. This tour includes a selection of real places associated with the life and work of August Wilson and both real and imagined places that are important in the plays of his Pittsburgh Cycle (see page 121 for summaries of the plays).

   Please note: If you expect to see the sites of all ten plays, you will be disappointed. *Ma Rainey's Black Bottom* is set in a Chicago recording studio. But even of the nine Hill plays, the site of *The Piano Lesson* is left vague and we can only make educated guesses for the locations of *Joe Turner's Come and Gone*, *Fences*, and *Radio Golf*. Locations of the other five plays are quite specific, although specific in different ways.

2. The tour route is highlighted on the map on pages 58–59.

3. Tour directions are given in bold italics. The route is about five miles. Walk, bike, or drive as you wish.

4. The current name of a place is given in the heading. Historical names are referred to in the text.

5. Architects and building dates (design-completion) are given when known. All the architects practiced in Pittsburgh, unless otherwise noted.

6. Local, state, and federal designations awarded to a place are noted. For information on the meaning of the designations, contact the Pittsburgh History & Landmarks Foundation: www.phlf.org; 412-471-5808.

7. The Carnegie Library of Pittsburgh's Hill District branch (see page 84) and Hill House Association (see page 97) are open to the public. If you plan on visiting, please check websites or contact each place in advance for days and hours of operation.

*Begin at Freedom Corner, at Centre Avenue and Crawford Street.
If you are arriving by bus, there is a Port Authority stop at that
intersection. If you are arriving by car and plan on walking, park
your car on either street, but do not park in the church parking lot.*

1. Freedom Corner Monument

*Centre Avenue and Crawford Street
Howard K. Graves, architect; sculpture by Carlos Peterson, 2001*

The Freedom Corner Monument has two concentric rings:
the Freedom Marchers ring contains the names of seventy
heroes of the local civil rights movement and the Circle of
Honor contains the names of twenty-five "fallen heroes"

who passed away
before the monument's
dedication. In the
center is a polished
granite "stone of origin"
from Zimbabwe, sym-
bolizing the origin and
power of the African
American heritage.
On the back wall is
the Spiritual Form,
cast in bronze, com-
memorating the courage of those who applied the principles
of nonviolence in the pursuit of human rights. Its sculptor,
Carlos Peterson, grew up nearby on Crawford Street.

The name Freedom Corner was established by 1965, when
it had become (as it remains) an assembly point for many
groups, white as well as black, marching downtown to protest
for social justice. Hill District Councilman Jake Milliones
proposed this civil rights monument, and the project was
realized in 2001 under the leadership of his successor,
Councilman Sala Udin.

Look west from Freedom Corner to the Lower Hill, sloping

toward downtown Pittsburgh. This area was drastically altered by urban renewal, beginning in 1956, and it is again the site of controversy and change as this guidebook goes to press in January 2011. The fate of the Civic/Mellon Arena—the large, domed structure designed in 1954 by Mitchell & Ritchey, completed in 1961, and in use until its closing on June 27, 2010—is uncertain. The Pittsburgh Penguins, a principal tenant of the arena, began moving out in mid-July to Consol Energy Center, a new facility across Centre Avenue.

The Civic Arena and its parking lots are where, during August Wilson's childhood, Logan and Fullerton streets crossed Bedford, Wylie, and Centre avenues. That was the commercial heart of the Hill, a vibrant, although run-down, multi-ethnic neighborhood crowded with stores, churches, synagogues, night clubs, bars, and produce and meat markets. *Fullerton Street* is the title of one of Wilson's early, unpublished plays. Logan Street, familiarily called "Jew Town," had sidewalk vendors as on New York's Lower East Side. Referred to in seven of Wilson's ten plays, Logan Street loomed large in his imagination; in *Seven Guitars*, Floyd recalls seeing Vera for the first time on Logan Street.

Starting in 1956, the Lower Hill was obliterated by the Urban Redevelopment Authority in an effort to create a civic auditorium and improved housing, as evidenced by Washington Plaza, the twenty-two-story cream-colored apartment building designed by I. M. Pei (New York) in 1958 and erected in 1964, across Crawford Street from Freedom Corner. Evicted Italians, Jews, and others moved elsewhere, but blacks largely moved into the Middle Hill and Homewood, creating overcrowding that soon led to deterioration. Blacks had initially supported redevelopment because they had been promised new housing. When this did not materialize, the community opposed further redevelopment and, in 1968, erected a billboard at this intersection that read: "NO Redevelopment Beyond This Point! We Demand Low Income Housing for the Lower Hill."

2. St. Benedict the Moor Church

91 Crawford Street
Henry Moeser, architect, 1893–95
Historic Landmark Plaque

Although the Kittel family was not Roman Catholic, Freddy Kittel (who became August Wilson) attended third and fourth grades at Holy Trinity School, 107–13 Fullerton Street. Holy Trinity School, parish hall, and nunnery—all on the west side of Crawford Street—were demolished in the late 1950s to make way for the Civic Arena (see map, page xvi).

This church carries on the legacy of four parishes. Originally known as Holy Trinity, the building housed a German congregation whose legacy is preserved in its fine Felgemaker organ. By the 1950s, the Catholic population of the Hill had dwindled to the point that the area could not support the number of existing parishes. On April 16, 1958, Holy Trinity merged with St. Brigid (see page 76; see map, page 79) and became St. Brigid Parish.

On May 14, 1968, the parish merged with St. Benedict the Moor, an African American parish established in 1889, and became St. Brigid-St. Benedict the Moor. The congregation erected the landmark statue of St. Benedict the Moor, designed by Frederick Shrady, with outstretched arms welcoming visitors to the Hill District—although August Wilson, among others, saw it as turning its back on the Hill since it faces downtown. In 1977, St. Brigid-St. Benedict the Moor merged with St. Richard's Church (see page 87) and the parish became St. Benedict the Moor.

Proceed north on Crawford Street and stop just beyond St. Benedict the Moor Church near the new housing.

3. Crawford Street (rented room; demolished)

In a rooming house on Crawford Street on April 1, 1965, soon after his father, also Frederick August Kittel, had died, Freddy Kittel renamed himself August Wilson. Using twenty dollars he earned writing a college term paper for one of his sisters, he purchased a typewriter downtown and carried it up the hill because he did not have any money left to take a bus. On a fresh sheet of paper he typed out possible names, combining his father's and mother's names—Freddy Kittel … August Kittel … Frederick August Wilson … August Wilson.

The first phase of housing you see here was built in 1992, followed by second and third phases in 1995 and 1999. These Crawford Square Apartments, designed by Urban Design Associates and funded by the Urban Redevelopment Authority of Pittsburgh, include 101 town homes and 247 apartments. They have attracted professionals, college students, and families back to the Lower Hill.

*Continue north to the end of Crawford Street at Bedford Avenue.
Look left (west).*

4. Connelley Trade School

1501 Bedford Avenue
Edward B. Lee, architect, 1928–30
National Register of Historic Places; Historic Landmark Plaque

This was Clifford B. Connelley Trade School, or Connelley Vo-Tech. August Wilson, fifteen, was a ninth grader here for a few months in Fall 1960, after racial taunting by white students drove him out of Central Catholic High School in Oakland the previous spring. He elected automotive repair, but those classes were full, so this voluminous reader was enrolled in sheet metal classes, where the teachers complained that he did not take care of the tools. He remembered that on October 13, the day the underdog Pirates beat the mighty Yankees to win the World Series, he was in detention at Connelley when the teacher said, "OK, y'all can go." So he went downtown to watch the wild celebration, "and I got home at

3:00 in the morning. I was just going around watching." Later, he noted that the police stood by, tolerating the crowds in the streets and cars over-turned, a very different response than the one they showed to the relatively peaceful marchers in the anti-racism and anti-war protests of the 1970s.

The Clifford B. Connelley Trade School opened in 1930, in a building

near the old Central High School. Considered one of the largest and most modern trade schools of the time, it offered classes to black and white students alike in subjects such as carpentry, plumbing, and automotive repair, as well as classes to recent immigrants in citizenship and English as a Second Language. Note the entrance with carved figures representing various trades. The school closed in 2004. In 2011, Pittsburgh Green Innovators plans to break ground on the first phase of redeveloping Connelley as a nonprofit center for green education, training, research, and business development.

Turn right (east) on Bedford Avenue.

5. Letsche Education Center

1527–33 Bedford Avenue
1905; Marion M. Steen, architect for addition, 1941
National Register of Historic Places; Historic Landmark Plaque

Generations of Hill District elementary school students attended Letsche. August Wilson attended pre-school, kindergarten, and first and second grades here. The Letsche School's original building, in the Classical Revival style, faces Cliff Street, behind Bedford. A 1941 addition with Art Deco detailing faces Bedford Avenue. In 1975, the elementary school closed and Letsche became a city-wide Alternative Learning Center for boys and pregnant girls who could not cope with regular high school.
It closed in 2004. Pittsburgh Green Innovators hopes to include the Letsche building in its campus.

6. St. George Syrian/Antiochian Orthodox Church

1539 Bedford Avenue
Built in 1917

In 1917, the Hill District's substantial Syrian, Lebanese, and Palestinian congregation began worshipping in this charming yellow brick church with an onion-shaped dome. In 1959, the congregation moved to Oakland. Several Protestant congregations worshipped here subsequently. The building is locally owned, and the chapel and community room in the basement are used from time to time. According to the owner, "August Wilson hung out on the front steps; how could he not? All the other kids did."

7. 1621 Bedford Avenue

This is the last residence of August Wilson's mother, Daisy Wilson, who died in 1983. Notice the elegant floral decoration in brick at the top of the façade and in stone at the windows.

In 1999, while working at the Pittsburgh Public Theater on the world premiere of *King Hedley II*, Wilson identified the backyard of 1621 Bedford as the site he had in mind for the play (see photo, page 120). The address 1621 also shows up in *Two Trains Running*, less as an actual address than an additional tribute to his mother.

8. 1710 Bedford Avenue

This was the home of Raymond Goldblum, dermatologist, the "Doc Goldblum" referred to in *Joe Turner's Come and Gone*, *Seven Guitars*, and *Fences*.

1712 (left) and 1710 (right)

9. 1712 Bedford Avenue

This was the last residence of August Wilson's maternal grandmother, Zonia (whose name is given to the young girl in *Joe Turner*), and was also the home of the "ghost" Wilson drew on for *The Piano Lesson*. Most importantly, it was the residence of prize fighter Charlie Burley and his wife, a friend of Wilson's mother, where she and sometimes her children visited amid times of relative affluence. Since Charlie Burley is one of the obvious prototypes for Troy Maxson, it is possible to consider the backyard at 1712 as the site for *Fences*.

10. 1725 Bedford Avenue

In their combination shop and residence, Johnny Butera had a watch repair business while his brother Frank repaired shoes. Johnny was born and lived here continuously except for a time during World War II. The Buteras, of Italian descent, were well liked by the Kittels and other black families, which perhaps explains why their business was not damaged during the 1968 riots. However, crime increased substantially thereafter and Frank was killed during a 1969 robbery. Johnny, who used to speak of his familiarity with the Kittel children, was killed in 2002, also during an apparent robbery.

The artwork on the façades of 1725 and 1727 Bedford Avenue is the result of the "Windows of Hope" partnership with the Historic Hill Institute and the City of Pittsburgh. August Wilson's nephew, Paul Ellis, owns these buildings (see pages 20–21).

11. 1727 Bedford Avenue (front and rear)

1886 (front); 1847 or earlier (rear)
Pennsylvania Historical and Museum Commission marker;
City of Pittsburgh Historic Structure

This is the most important site in the Hill District life of Frederick August Kittel, Jr., who grew up to become August Wilson. At the rear of the building is the small apartment, originally an 1840s house, where August lived from his birth in 1945 to 1958, when the family moved to Hazelwood. During that time, Beatrice (Bella) Siger operated a market in the front building, originally constructed in 1886 by John F. E. Dorow. The Sigers were a Jewish family, prominent in the grocery business. Bella and her husband, Louis, opened Bella's Market in the building storefront in 1940. Louis died in 1945, but Bella continued operating the market and purchased the building in 1949 from grocer Morris Picovsky. Bella's Market closed around 1965 and 1727 Bedford Avenue was sold by Bella's estate after her death in 1970.

One or more of the Kittel children (memories differ) helped out informally in Bella's Market, especially when neighborhood children came in to buy candy.

August was the fourth child and first son of Daisy Wilson, who went on to have two more sons. The children, in order: Freda, Linda Jean, Donna, Frederick (August), Edwin, and Richard. (Barbara, a fourth daughter, was raised by others.) Their father, Frederick August Kittel, a German immigrant and skilled baker, lived with them intermittently.

Mother and children lived in two small rooms at the rear of 1727, accessible first by a narrow walkway (still evident) between it and the buildings that then filled what is now a vacant lot, then up the half-flight of stairs which is still there. Several years after Freddy's birth, the family expanded into the two rooms on the floor above. This whole site is that used in *Seven Guitars*, set in 1948 and located in what Wilson remembered of this back-yard, with the rear of the house in the background, and including characters (Louise and Hedley) named for residents of other rooms.

Looking at the house and yard, you can imagine the setting of Wilson's childhood, or at least feel as if you are on the set of *Seven Guitars*. Facing the back of the house, you can see the cellar door where in the play Hedley lives; looking through the large tree that has grown up, you can see the arch-way where there was a staircase leading to Louise's apartment. Whatever else Wilson's childhood was like, he remembered that backyard fondly as the place where his mother and the neighbors would bring out chairs and a radio and play cards, much like the vivid communal life in the play.

Explore the block south of Bedford to see site 12 by proceeding south on Roberts Street and right (west) on Webster Avenue to Manilla Street.

12. 1600 Block Webster Avenue/Manilla Street

This area is the probable location of the Holly boarding house, the setting of *Joe Turner's Come and Gone*. In the play, Herald Loomis is seen "standing up there on the corner watching the house … right up there on Manilla Street." Elsewhere in the play, there are references to "up on Bedford" and "down on Wylie." These clues fit Webster Avenue and the way the Hill District slopes down to the southwest. Ignore the modern houses: the area would have looked very different in 1911.

Proceed up (north on) Manilla Street to Bedford Avenue. Turn right (east) on Bedford and continue to Ledlie Street. Turn left (north) on Ledlie and continue to Cliff Street.

13. Loendi Club

(demolished)

Ledlie Street, between Cliff and Arcena Streets

New housing is on the site where the second home of the Loendi Club was located. Founded in 1897, the Loendi Club was Pittsburgh's oldest and most prestigious club for black men. Named for a river in Africa, it was first located at 83 Fullerton, in the heart of the Lower Hill, until urban redevelopment forced it to relocate here to Ledlie Street. Its elegant balls, dinners, and symposia

The Loendi Club on Ledlie Street, c. 1960–70.

set the tone for black Pittsburgh's business, professional, and social elite—but not too elite for the clever Canewell to win a raffle there in *Seven Guitars.* In the 1970s, the club declined in exclusivity and it closed in 1986.

Continue north on Ledlie Street to Arcena Street. Turn left (west) on Arcena and cross over to the green space.

14. Arcena Street View
Green space adjacent to 1703 Arcena Street

This is one of the great panoramic views from the Hill (see photos, page 74). Look west toward downtown Pittsburgh and the Ohio River valley, then east and down (literally) to the Strip District and Lawrenceville, then north across the Allegheny River to Pittsburgh's Northside. Near the top of the embankment are remnants of the piers of the Penn Incline (opened in 1884, demolished in 1956), which connected generations of Hill residents with the Strip District below.

In *Gem of the Ocean*, Solly says, "There's a Great Dane up on Arcena Street." And in *Two Trains Running,* Hambone had been "staying up there on Arcena Street," according to Holloway.

Looking northwest from Arcena Street across the Allegheny River to the Northside and Ohio River Valley beyond.

Looking down on the Strip District and northeast along the Allegheny River Valley. Notice the Penn Incline piers.

Follow Arcena Street back to Ledlie Street and return to Bedford Avenue. Turn left (east) on Bedford. Cross Bedford at Devilliers Street and look northeast.

15. Miller African Centered Academy

2055 Bedford Avenue
Carlton Strong, architect; designed in 1911, opened in 1916
Historic Landmark Plaque

During August Wilson's time, this Pittsburgh Public School was called McKelvy Elementary. In *King Hedley II*, Tonya mentions that Pernell's son goes to McKelvy School.

During the 1920s, McKelvy was used as a school during the day and as an educational and community center in the evening, serving immigrants who received basic instruction in citizenship. McKelvy Field, just behind the school, hosted many baseball teams in the 1920s, including the Pittsburgh Crawfords before they became professional. In 1985, McKelvy became a district Gifted Elementary School, and in 2006 it became the new home of Miller African Centered Academy for students in pre-school through fifth grade.

From Bedford Avenue and Devilliers Street, proceed down (south on)
Devilliers to Enoch Street. Turn right (west) on Enoch Street and
proceed to Granville Street. Turn left (south) on Granville and
continue to Wylie Avenue. Turn right (west) on Wylie. Proceed past
1845 Wylie (Nazareth Baptist Church) to the green space.

16. Aunt Ester's House (imagined)

1839 Wylie Avenue

The logic of house numbers would place Aunt Ester's house
in the green space next to 1845 Wylie Avenue. (Although a
vibrant, quirky, heroic character on her own, Aunt Ester stands
for *an-cestor*—say it aloud and see.) The house is fictitious,
although the location has a logical explanation. August Wilson
chose Wylie Avenue because that was the main street of the
black Hill, and he chose 1839 because that was the date of the
famous Amistad slave ship revolt. More personally, Wilson
would have known this sloping hillside since it was part of
the property belonging to St. Brigid's Church (Henry Moeser,
architect, 1871–72). Miss Sarah Degree, a neighborhood
woman, took Wilson to St. Brigid's Church as a child (see
map, page 79). Wilson also knew this as the front yard of the

HARMOND: [Aunt Ester's house is] a Federalist brick house with a good double-base foundation. I couldn't believe it. It has beveled glass on every floor. There's a huge stained-glass window leading up to the landing. And the staircase is made of Brazilian wood with a hand-carved balustrade. You don't see that too often. …

HARMOND: You should feel the woodwork. If you run your hand slow over some of the wood you can make out these carvings. There's faces. Lines making letters. An old language. And there's this smell in the air. …

HARMOND: … The air in the house smells sweet like a new day.

Radio Golf: Act Two, Scene 2

Ozanam Cultural Center (1833 Wylie Avenue), operated by the Catholic Diocese for Hill District youth from 1970 to 1997. Wilson considered cultural centers and theater spaces as important as churches.

1839 Wylie is an eloquent empty space in which to recover Wilson's poetic myth-making. This is the site of *Gem of the Ocean*, where the August Wilson century begins. It is where Holloway, Memphis, Sterling, and West visit Aunt Ester (all but the last to great effect) in *Two Trains Running*. It is where she dies in *King Hedley II*, after being visited by the prophet Stool Pigeon and the martyr King. And, as the century ends, it is at the center of the conflict in *Radio Golf*: the crumbling mansion has become the neglected soul of the Hill, about to be torn down. Or is it the site where a new Aunt Ester has already been born?

To those with imagination, 1839 Wylie is actually more real than real. By looking at this site, you can imagine yourself

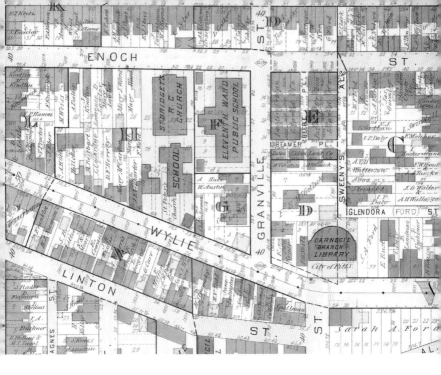

A map from 1906 shows the open space facing Wylie (just above the "W" in Wylie), where Aunt Ester's house is imagined to be. St. Brigid's R. C. Church and School face Enoch Street. On the map, published by Hopkins in Philadelphia, St. Brigid's is incorrectly spelled "St. Bridget's." St. Brigid's was torn down in 1961. Notice the Wylie Avenue Carnegie branch library, now The First Muslim Mosque of Pittsburgh (see page 80).

visiting Aunt Ester. The view from the top of the green space looks southward toward the Monongahela Valley, once the heart of Pittsburgh's iron- and steel-making industry, toward those far-away southern states where most blacks in Pittsburgh or their forebears (certainly most in Wilson's plays) began their migration northward. This hillside is haunted by the spirits of August Wilson, Aunt Ester, and all the questing men and women they imagined and served.

Proceed east on Wylie Avenue, back to Granville Street.
Continue on Wylie to the next site.

17. The First Muslim Mosque of Pittsburgh

1911 Wylie Avenue
Alden & Harlow, architects, 1899

During August Wilson's childhood, this was the Wylie Avenue branch of the Carnegie Library of Pittsburgh. The library name is faintly visible above the entrance arch. This is where August Wilson, age five, received his treasured first library card. One of his mother's enduring gifts was to teach him to read when he was four, which he called transforming: "You can unlock information and you're better able to understand the forces that are oppressing you."

The Wylie Avenue branch of the Carnegie Library housed some 200,000 books in fifteen languages, with an especially large collection in Yiddish, the language of the Hill's largest ethnic group, Russian Jews, at the time of the library's opening. By the 1940s, as blacks constituted an increasing majority of the Hill's population, the library's foreign-language collection was replaced with an increasingly black-oriented collection. In 1982, the library relocated to Dinwiddie Street near Centre Avenue—and then, in 2008, to a new building at the corner of Centre Avenue and Kirkpatrick Street (see page 84).

In 1984, the First Muslim Mosque (Al-Masjid Al-Awwal), an orthodox Sunni mosque, acquired the building. The First Muslim Mosque was chartered in 1932 by indigenous American

Muslims and is the oldest mosque in Pennsylvania.

Continue east on Wylie past Devilliers Street to Erin Street. (Just past Devilliers, opposite Ebenezer Baptist Church, notice the Wylie Avenue façade of the Pythian Temple/New Granada. See photo, page 95.)

18. Westbrook Jitney Station

2046 Wylie Avenue

This building stands as an example of the many jitney stations that were needed because taxis would not service the Hill. It is popularly referred to as the Wylie and Erin Jitney Station.

Sala Udin (then Sam Howze) says that he, August Wilson, and Rob Penny often met at the Pan Fried Fish restaurant operated by two brothers, Clifford and Irv, on Wylie Avenue near Arthur and Roberts streets. Wilson typically arrived before the others and passed the time at a jitney station next door, listening to the drivers brag and laugh, telling stories both true and invented.

Similarly, in *Jitney*, the men keep going next door to Clifford's to get a fish sandwich. The building Wilson frequented had disappeared by the time he wrote *Jitney*, and there are three other jitney stations mentioned in the play, but this one at 2046 Wylie Avenue can stand as the site of the play because its telephone number, 412-566-9802, recalls the number of the vanished station, Court 1-9802. If you are invited inside, you will see it looks just like the stage set Wilson describes, with the exception of the television set. The old-fashioned pay telephone still rings constantly.

Continue east on Wylie Avenue, past The Legacy senior housing (see page 53), to Elmore Street.

19. Crawford Grill No. 2

2141 Wylie Avenue
Pennsylvania Historical and Museum Commission marker

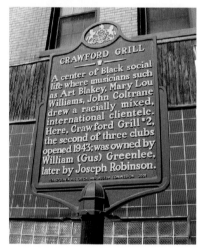

This night spot, located in the Middle Hill, opened in 1943 as a companion to Grill No. 1 in the Lower Hill. Like its namesake, Grill No. 2 was a center for live music, good food, and a conviviality that attracted an interracial clientele. Crawford Grill is mentioned in both *Fences* and *King Hedley II*. Both grills were established by Gus Greenlee, numbers king of the Hill and owner of the Pittsburgh Crawfords baseball team. Grill No. 1 closed in 1952 as urban renewal threatened. Grill No. 2, owned by Joseph Robinson, became the jazz epicenter of the Hill, along with the Hurricane Lounge. The Grill closed in 2002. In 2010, a group of investors, including former Pittsburgh Steeler Franco Harris, bought the building with the intention of reopening it as a jazz club.

Continue east on Wylie Avenue to Kirkpatrick Street.

20. Eddie's Restaurant (demolished)

2172 Wylie Avenue

This small eatery was a favorite haunt of August Wilson's, where he regularly hung out, writing poetry while stretching a cup of coffee. Eddie was always an indulgent proprietor, even letting some clients run a tab. Sala Udin has recalled that the rear booth served as a regular meeting place, practically an office, for himself, August, and playwright Rob Penny during the days of their Black Horizon Theater. Other artistic friends who

Eddie's Restaurant, c. 1950–75

hung out there included Maisha Baton and Bob Johnson, who both taught at the University of Pittsburgh. Reportedly, Wilson conceived the idea of *Jitney*, the first he wrote of his Pittsburgh Cycle plays, at Eddie's Restaurant.

Eddie's is mentioned in *The Piano Lesson*, but the play with the strongest connections to it is *Two Trains Running*, set in 1969 in a fictional but similar diner, Memphis Lee's, located somewhere in the immediate vicinity, probably just across Kirkpatrick Street. In *Two Trains Running* there is also much mention of Lutz's Meat Market, located in a still-surviving building on Centre Avenue at Elmore (see page 89), and the West Funeral Home, located at 2215 Wylie (see page 84). Late in the play, the address of Memphis's diner is given as 1621 Wylie, but that doesn't fit with the other evidence. That number honors Wilson's mother, who lived her final years at 1621 Bedford (see page 68). All this detail notwithstanding, the atmosphere of Memphis's diner is pure Eddie's.

Carnegie Library of Pittsburgh's Hill District branch, 2177 Centre Avenue

Eddie's was torn down in 2006 to make space for the parking lot behind the new Hill District branch of the Carnegie Library of Pittsburgh, designed by Pfaffmann + Associates and opened in 2008. In symbolic recompense, a counter stool from Eddie's is installed in the new library's "living room" (see photo, page 134), where there is a large 1923 map of the Hill on which the conjectured locations of the Pittsburgh Cycle plays are marked. The library is a pleasant place for a mid-tour pause.

Continue east on Wylie past Kirkpatrick Street to Belinda Street.

21. West Funeral Home

2215 Wylie Avenue

This building was erected in 1970 by Thomas L. West, Jr., and Raymond West, as a memorial to their parents, Thomas L. West, Sr., and Nellie West. Thomas L. West, Sr., the founder, was a retired

postal worker who in 1932 opened West Funeral Home at 2216 Centre Avenue, near Kirkpatrick Street. It soon became one of the Hill District's leading funeral homes. It is mentioned in *The Piano Lesson*, but both it and West himself are featured in *Two Trains Running*. There, West appears as a tight-fisted, practical commentator on neighborhood affairs—the only character in the cycle based directly on a real Pittsburgh person.

Continue east on Wylie Avenue to Somers Street. Turn left (north) on Somers and continue all the way up to Bedford Avenue. Turn right (east) on Bedford Avenue and continue past the state historical marker for Greenlee Field, to just beyond Morgan Street.

22. Tuberculosis League Hospital Historic District

Janssen & Abbott, architects, 1915–17; E. P. Mellon (New York), architect, 1921, 1929, 1940; Ingham, Boyd & Pratt, architects, 1949
2851 Bedford Avenue
National Register of Historic Places

August Wilson would have passed these eight buildings, formerly the Tuberculosis League Hospital, when he walked to St. Richard's School (see page 87), which he attended from September 1955 to 1958. The hospital is mentioned in *Seven Guitars*, set in 1948:

> LOUISE: Hedley got TB and don't want to go into the sanitarium. He got this letter from the board of health telling him to be down there on Thursday. I called down there and told them. They want him to come down and get tested.

The former Dispensary of 1940 (top) and the former Nurses Home of 1949 (above).

85

Tuberculosis League Hospital of 1929, now Milliones Manor.

CANEWELL: They letting colored in the sanitarium now. They got one right up there on Bedford. They moved all the white people out and it's sitting there half empty. They looking to fill it up. He ought to go on and let them take him. He can get well.

The historic buildings c. 1912–49 are primarily Italian Romanesque Revival in style, with the exception of Janssen & Abbott's Renaissance Revival Children's Building. Several health agencies are located here and three buildings provide senior citizen housing, including the main hospital building of 1929 (Milliones Manor). Follow the road on the east side of Western Manor (the former Nurses Home of 1949) and walk through the complex, beautifully sited on a hilltop, where the air and peaceful setting would have provided comfort to the TB patients.

Two blocks west, at Bedford Avenue and Francis Street, August Wilson would also have passed the site of the Municipal Hospital of Infectious and Contagious Diseases

(Sidney F. Heckert, architect, 1903–04) at 2631 Bedford Avenue. This facility relocated to the University of Pittsburgh campus c. 1940. (In 1957 the Oakland building was given to the University and renamed Jonas Salk Hall.) 2631 Bedford Avenue is now Francis Street Community Garden and Urban Farm.

Continue a short distance on Bedford Avenue to Wandless Street.

23. St. Benedict the Moor School

2900 Bedford Avenue

Originally St. Richard's R. C. Church and School, this Italian Renaissance Revival building was constructed in 1907–08 and dedicated May 24, 1908. The first floor housed the church and the second floor housed the school. Although the parish intended to build a new church and convert the entire building into a school, this never happened. In 1977, St. Richard's merged with St. Brigid and St. Benedict the Moor, and the parish adopted the latter name. The former St. Richard's became St. Benedict the Moor School.

August Wilson attended third grade through the first part of seventh here at St. Richard's. On May 30, 1989, Wilson visited the school and told the students that his sixth-grade teacher, Sister Christopher, was the first teacher who encouraged him to write.

Follow Bedford Avenue west back to Kirkpatrick Street/Memory Lane, just past the state historical marker for Josh Gibson. Turn left (south) on Kirkpatrick Street and continue to Centre Avenue. Turn left (east) on Centre and proceed to Soho Street.

24. Pittsburgh Weil School

2250 Centre Avenue
Marion M. Steen, architect, 1942
Historic Landmark Plaque

This school, A. Leo Weil, was named for a prominent Pittsburgh lawyer, Adolphus Leo Weil (1858–1938). In 1968, playwright Rob Penny, poet August Wilson, and actor Sala Udin (among others) established the Black Horizon Theater in the school's auditorium, performing plays by such black playwrights as Amiri Baraka, Ed Bullins, and eventually Penny. Since no one else was prepared to direct, Wilson volunteered. He tells how he went to the library to find a book on directing. He did not

realize that the co-author of this standard text was Lawrence Carra, a professor at Carnegie Mellon University, just a few miles away.

Architect Marion M. Steen was hired by the Board of Education in 1935, in the midst of the Depression, to design school buildings and supervise their construction. His Art Deco school buildings include Prospect on Mt. Washington (1931/1936), Burgwin in Hazelwood (1937), Carmalt in Brookline

(1937), Thaddeus Stevens in Elliott (1940), and Letsche (1941) and A. Leo Weil (1942) in the Hill District.

Continue back (west) on Centre Avenue, past Kirkpatrick Street and the Carnegie Library's Hill District branch, to Elmore Street.

25. Lutz's Meat Market

2145 Centre Avenue

The store name is still visible at the top of the building, just below the cornice. Lutz is an important off-stage character in *Two Trains Running* who bilks Hambone of his promised ham as payment for painting his fence. When Risa says, "Lutz gonna rot in hell," Wolf replies, "Lutz gonna go to hell with a ham under each arm." But the popularity of this white-owned butcher shop, in existence at least by 1941, is attested by a 1950 society column in the *Pittsburgh Courier*: "This week, Lutz's market had the delectable smell of frying sausage meat … succulent with spices tickling your nostrils … so that you practically drooled over the counter." Lutz was also

active in the community: the 1960 Lutz Market bowling team tied for first place in the Dapper Dan charity bowling tournament. But, however well liked by some, his market was burned and looted during the riots of 1968, after which he sold the business to Cal Cunningham, a black employee.

Continue west on Centre Avenue to see sites 26 through 32.

26. Ellis Hotel (demolished)

2044 Centre Avenue

The Ellis Hotel, once at the corner of Centre Avenue and Addison Street where the vacant lot is now, shows up as a place of assignation in three August Wilson plays. Shealy, the numbers runner in *Jitney*, goes there hoping to meet the right woman, and, in *Two Trains Running*, Wolf, also a numbers runner, reports that Petey Brown caught his "old lady" there with his best friend and killed them both. In *King Hedley II*, King's mother, Ruby, says that when she first realized she had gray hair, she went with a man to the Ellis Hotel for a night of rough sex; then in the morning she told herself, "I'm still a woman. Gray hair and all."

The Ellis Hotel was begun by James and Frank Ellis on the South Side, then moved in 1951 to Reed Street in the Hill, and in 1957 into the former black YWCA at this site. Back when blacks were turned away from white hotels, the Ellis welcomed celebrities like Jackie Robinson, Miles Davis, Nina Simone, and Ray Charles. In the 1970s, it fell on hard times, and, by 1980, it had become a residence for seniors. It closed in 1995 after a fire, and in 2002 the abandoned building, then a notorious drug den, was torn down.

27. Halfway Art Gallery (demolished)

2033 Centre Avenue at Calliope Way

Another vacant lot marks the spot of the Halfway Art Gallery. August Wilson recalled the place in a 1987 interview:

Then, around 1967, there was this art gallery, Halfway Art Gallery, in Pittsburgh. It was a place to congregate. We put out a little magazine called Signal. *Then we changed the name to* Connection. *I was the Poetry Editor. Then we decided to name ourselves the Centre Avenue Poets Theater Workshop. We had poetry readings and gallery jazz sessions and the whole bit. We talked about doing theater, 'cause theater was part of our name. I had never seen a play before.*

The former art gallery and community center was headed by Ed "Ewari" Ellis, local artist and activist in Pittsburgh's Black Arts Movement of the 1960s. The gallery was funded as part of the Hill District Project of St. Stephen's Episcopal Church of Sewickley, whose pastor, Reverend Richard Martin, had his offices at the gallery. The gallery sponsored art work by Ellis and other local artists, as well as poetry readings by persons such as Chawley Williams and dancing and drumming by local and national groups. Sala Udin, a long-time friend of Ellis, considered Halfway as more than an art gallery; it was "a political center for the new African Cultural Consciousness-Black Power movement in Pittsburgh." It closed in 1974 or 1975.

The Hill CDC (center) is located where Irv's Bar once was.

28. Hill Community Development Corporation

2015–17 Centre Avenue

This handsome brick building is now home to the Hill District Community Development Corporation (CDC), a nonprofit, grassroots community organization focusing on housing and commercial development in the Hill District. It has been a major player in promoting the redevelopment of the Hill, largely through the construction and rehabilitation of homes and businesses, such as the Hill Phoenix Shopping Center at 1860 Centre Avenue and town houses on several Hill sites.

Irv's Bar opened here in 1959, serving "Hot Fish Sandwiches, Hamburgers, Kosher Corned Beef, and Salami." It made a large impression on August Wilson, who refers to it in four plays. In *Seven Guitars* and *Jitney* those references are in passing, but in *Two Trains Running* Irv's is noted as dangerous:

> STERLING: I just got out the penitentiary. I was down at Irv's yesterday. But I figure [if] I hang out down there I'll be right back down the penitentiary.

In *King Hedley II,* this is where King kills Purnell: "I saw Purnell going into Irv's bar. He went straight back to the phone booth. I don't know who he was calling but that was the last call he made."

Of course that's fiction, but in real life Irv's had a mixed reputation. Domenick Calabrese, former tavern owner, told *Pittsburgh Courier* columnist John Clark in 1959, "I worried myself sick trying to figure out when [the patrons] were going to fight, shoot, or cut each other." However, the new owner, Irving Singer, disputed that assessment. In 1960 Clark praised the bar under Singer's ownership and management and included it among drinking places along Centre Avenue that "display a spirit of warmth and welcome." Intriguingly, Irv is the name of Ma's white manager in *Ma Rainey's Black Bottom.*

Centre Avenue, March 21, 1961. Notice the "DA" from the New Granada sign and, beyond, the "RV'S" from the Irv's Bar sign.

29. New Granada Theater

2007 Centre Avenue
Louis A. S. Bellinger, architect, 1927–28
Alfred M. Marks, architect for remodeling, 1936–37
National Register of Historic Places; City of Pittsburgh Historic
Structure; Historic Landmark Plaque

August Wilson would have known this building, one of the
largest and most prominent secular buildings in the Hill
District, as the New Granada Theater, a movie palace, live

entertainment venue, and community
events center that opened on May 20,
1937. The New Granada was a remodeling of the Pythian Temple, a black
fraternal lodge commissioned ten
years earlier by the Grand Lodge of
the Knights of Pythias and designed
by Louis Arnett Stuart Bellinger
(1891–1946), Pittsburgh's first African

The Wylie Avenue façade in 1935. The inscription above the door, still visible today, reads: "Pythian Temple A.D. 1927."

American architect. Bellinger also designed Greenlee Field in the Hill, home of the celebrated Pittsburgh Crawfords professional baseball team in the 1930s. He was one of three black architects invited to participate in the first exhibition of African American art in the United States (sponsored by the Harmon Foundation in New York City in 1928).

Hendel Theater Corporation oversaw conversion of the Pythian Temple into the New Granada Theater. Architect Alfred M. Marks converted the vast first-floor "drill hall" into a movie theater. The second-floor auditorium had hosted black musicians after the Pythian Temple opened in 1928, including Louis Armstrong, Duke Ellington, and Cab Callaway, and the New Granada management continued to book leading black bands and artists. By the late 1930s, the auditorium was known as the Savoy Ballroom, named for a famous Harlem dance hall that opened in 1926. The second Savoy Ballroom opened in Chicago in 1927, and the third opened in Pittsburgh at 2314 Centre Avenue on Christmas Eve 1933.

In *Two Trains Running*, set in 1969, Sterling asks Risa to go with him to a rally to celebrate Malcolm X's birthday, "right down there at the Savoy Ballroom. They might have some dancing. You like to dance?" Risa replies, "If it be with the right person."

The Hill Community Development Corporation (the building owner), African American architect Milton Ogot, and Pittsburgh History & Landmarks Foundation collaborated on a $1.1 million stabilization of the New Granada in 2007–10, funded by The Heinz Endowments, the Commonwealth of Pennsylvania, and Allegheny County. The first-floor façade is Art Deco, dating from the 1936–37 remodeling; its polychromatic marquee has been removed for restoration. The upper floors retain their original fraternal decoration.

From Centre Avenue and Devilliers Street, look south.

30. Workingmen's Civic Club (demolished)

407 Devilliers Street

Ebenezer Tower is about where the Workingmen's Civic Club once was. Well known for live music and entertainment, it was especially popular in the 1960s when August Wilson would have gone there. It is mentioned in *Joe Turner's Come and Gone, Seven Guitars, Two Trains Running,* and *Jitney,* all but the first in connection with music. *Jitney* has this exchange:

PHILMORE: I went down the Workmen's Club. They had
Kenny Fisher down there. You couldn't hardly get in.
I ain't never seen so many people. You used to have to
have a job to get in there.

SHEALY: I know they glad they changed that rule. Wouldn't
nobody be down there.

PHILMORE: I'd be down there. I got me a job.

31. Hill House Association

1835 Centre Avenue
Walter L. Roberts, Jr., architect, 1971–73

In a series of amusing
conversations in *Radio Golf*,
Harmond Wilks, real estate
developer and mayoral can-
didate, tells Old Joe to go
down to Hill House to get a
lawyer if he wants to save his
house from the wrecking
ball. Old Joe resists because
he says, "They tell you, 'Sit
over there and wait.' 'Fill out this paper.' 'Turn over.' 'Jump up
and down.' I tried to tell them I wasn't no dog but they wasn't
listening. Told me to go down to the Animal Rescue Society
if I wanted a license for my dog. I told them I wanted to see
a lawyer. They told me, 'Fill out this form. ...' "

Playwriting aside, Hill House Association houses health
and human services agencies. The building opened in 1973,
on the site of the Irene Kaufmann Settlement House (1909–11).
Hill House was designed by African American architect
Walter Lenox Roberts, Jr. (1908–82). Born in Cambridge,
Massachusetts, Roberts received a B.A. in industrial design
from Carnegie Institute of Technology (now Carnegie Mellon
University) in 1937. He left Pittsburgh but returned after
World War II, apprenticed with local architectural firms,

and became a registered architect in 1953. He established his firm in 1959. Roberts later taught architecture and mechanical engineering at Pittsburgh Technical Institute and Carnegie Mellon University.

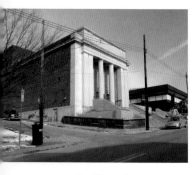

32. Kaufmann Auditorium

1835 Centre Avenue
Edward Stotz, architect, 1928–30
Historic Landmark Plaque

The Kaufmann Auditorium, operated by Hill House Association, is the sole surviving building of the Irene Kaufmann Settlement. The Settlement shows up significantly in two August Wilson plays. In *The Piano Lesson*, set in 1936, Berniece and Avery drop off young Maretha there for "extra school" on their way downtown by streetcar to arrange a loan. In preparation, Berniece admonishes her daughter, "You mind them people down there. Don't be going down there showing your color." And in *Jitney*, set in 1977, the gossipy Turnbo mentions it twice, most importantly as one in a list of the failed promises of Hill reconstruction: "They supposed to build another part to the Irene Kaufman [*sic*] Settlement House to replace the part they tore down."

The Irene Kaufmann Settlement was established in 1908 as a social service agency to assist Jewish residents of the Hill. A $150,000 building, designed by Charles Bickel, opened in 1911 and was dedicated to the memory of Irene Kaufmann, daughter of Kaufmann Department Store Vice-President Henry M. Kaufmann. In 1930, a $635,000 addition, designed in 1928 by architect Edward Stotz, was joined to the 1911 Settlement House. The new building consisted of the Theresa L. Kaufmann Auditorium (named in memory of Henry Kaufmann's

Only the auditorium portion (far left) of the Irene Kaufmann Settlement, shown here on November 12, 1940, remains. The addition (middle) and Settlement House (right) were demolished in 1968.

wife and decorated with stone and plaster work by Pittsburgh sculptor Frank Vittor) and an addition with music and art studios, classrooms, and a gymnasium with a swimming pool with blue tiles designed by Joseph Urban of New York.

In 1943, the Irene Kaufmann Settlement opened a branch facility in Squirrel Hill to serve recent European immigrants. When many Jewish residents in the Hill also moved to Squirrel Hill in the 1950s, the Settlement moved there permanently. In 1957, the Settlement donated the Centre Avenue Kaufmann Settlement buildings to the black community and the name was changed to the Anna B. Heldman Community Center. Heldman closed in 1964, and, in 1968, the Settlement House and addition were razed to make way for Hill House Association, a new community center that would consolidate neighborhood social services.

Continue west on Centre Avenue and you will come to Freedom Corner, where the tour began. Comments? info@phlf.org

Pittsburgh Area Map

1. St. Stephen's R. C. School and Church
2. Carnegie Library of Pittsburgh, Hazelwood
3. Gladstone School
4. Carnegie Library of Pittsburgh, Main (Oakland)
5. Soldiers and Sailors Memorial Hall and Museum
6. Central Catholic High School
7. 5822 Alder Street
8. New Hazlett Theater
9. O'Reilly Theater (Pittsburgh Public Theater)
10. August Wilson Center for African American Culture
11. Allegheny County Courthouse and Former Jail
12. State Correctional Institution at Pittsburgh
13. Greenwood Cemetery

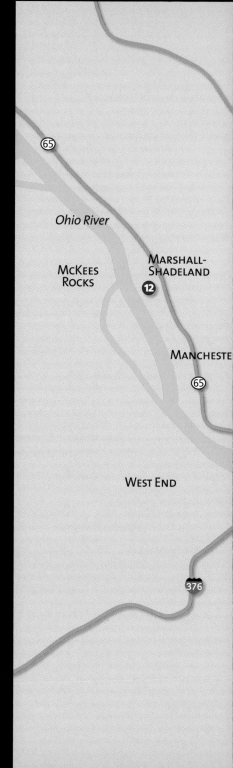

Ohio River

MCKEES ROCKS

MARSHALL-SHADELAND

MANCHESTE

WEST END

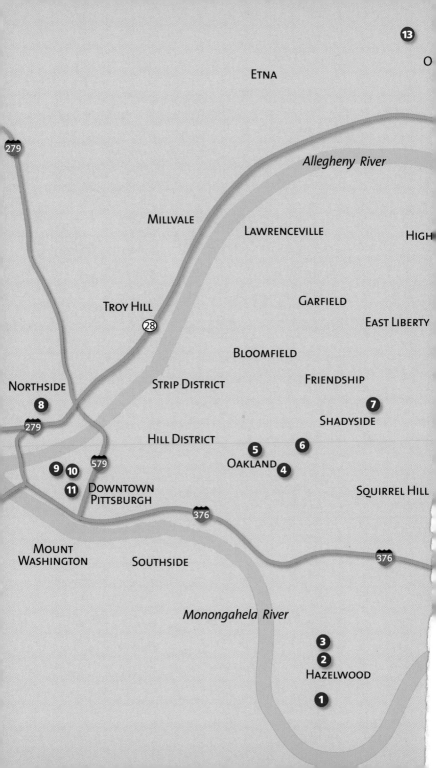

STOOL PIGEON: ... I'm gonna get you some fish heads
tomorrow. I got to go down to the Strip District.
Used to have the live fish market right down there
on Centre. Times ain't nothing like they used to be.
Everything done got broke up. Pieces flying
everywhere. ...

The people wandering all over the place. They got
lost. They don't even know the story of how they
got from tit to tat. Aunt Ester know. But the path to
her house is all grown over with weeds, you can't
hardly find the door no more. The people need to
know that. The people need to know the story.
See how they fit into it. See what part they play.

KING HEDLEY II: PROLOGUE

Tour of Sites Beyond the Hill

General Notes

1. Here is a selection of places in Pittsburgh (beyond the Hill) important in August Wilson's life or noted in the plays of his Pittsburgh Cycle (see page 121 for summaries of the plays).

2. The sites are located on the map on pages 100–101. Addresses are given for each site in the following text so you can find specific driving directions on your own.

3. The current name of a place is given in the heading. Historical names are referred to in the text.

4. Architects and building dates (design-completion) are given when known. All the architects practiced in Pittsburgh, unless otherwise noted.

5. Local, state, and federal designations awarded to a place are noted. For information on the meaning of the designations, contact the Pittsburgh History & Landmarks Foundation: www.phlf.org; 412-471-5808.

6. Sites 4, 5, 10, 11, and 13 are open to the public. If you plan on visiting, please check websites or contact each place in advance for specific information (admission fees and days/hours of operation).

1. St. Stephen's R. C. School and Church

131 Elizabeth Street, Hazelwood
School, 1910; architect unknown; addition, late 1930s
Church, Frederick C. Sauer, architect, 1902–03; rebuilt 1925,
A. F. Link & Associates, architects

In 1958, Daisy Wilson moved her family to Hazelwood and
enrolled the future playwright in the school at St. Stephen's
Parish, where he finished the seventh grade and stayed
through the eighth. The Italian Renaissance school stands
up the hill behind the grand Spanish Renaissance church.

2. Carnegie Library of Pittsburgh, Hazelwood

4748 Monongahela Street, Hazelwood
Alden & Harlow, architects, 1900
City of Pittsburgh Historic Structure

If August Wilson's self-education began in 1950 in the Carnegie
Library on Wylie Avenue in the Hill, it continued at the
Carnegie Library in Hazelwood. Wilson wrote in 1999:

> *When I was fourteen, I walked into the Hazelwood Branch*
> *of the Carnegie Library on my way home from Louis Field*
> *with my basketball under my arm and changed my life.*

I discovered the Negro section of the library with its thirty or so books. Before I was to discover Langston Hughes and Richard Wright and Ralph Ellison, I discovered an obscure sociological text in which I came across the phrase "the Negro's power of hard work." … The word power was magical. I had never seen or heard of it associated with the word Negro before. … I wrenched it from its place in the text and set it separate in my mind in a high place. … But one thing I took beyond all others that that shelf of books gave me was the proof that it was possible to be a writer. I decided that that is what I wanted to be. …

The Carnegie branch libraries were designed between 1898 and 1903 by Alden & Harlow, then Pittsburgh's leading architectural firm. Pittsburgh's Carnegie branch libraries were the first in the nation, and often served as community cultural centers—book stacks and reading rooms were usually complemented by an auditorium for lectures, meetings, and musical performances: Hazelwood's could seat 250.

In 2004, Carnegie Library of Pittsburgh relocated the Hazelwood branch to 4901 Second Avenue, leaving this historic structure closed and unused.

3. Gladstone School

327 Hazelwood Avenue, Hazelwood
O. M. Topp, architect, 1914; 1923–26

After his unhappy ninth grade at Central Catholic in Oakland and an aborted few months at Connelley Trade School in the Hill, August Wilson returned to Hazelwood (which shows up in *Gem of the Ocean*) and attended Gladstone High School in Winter-Spring 1961. There he was famously accused by a black teacher—"one of those black teachers who did not like black people," as Wilson said—of plagiarizing a twenty-page paper on Napoleon. He dropped out, and when the school personnel did not seem to care, he never returned. It was the last of his formal education.

Built in two stages, Gladstone climbs the steep hillside along Hazelwood Avenue between Sylvan Avenue and Gladstone Street, near where Daisy Wilson's family lived. Its architect, O. M. Topp, was born and educated in Norway. He lived and worked in Pittsburgh from 1888 to 1945. Although Topp designed many churches and commercial buildings, Gladstone may be his only school design. Gladstone closed in 2001; still owned by the Pittsburgh Board of Public Education in 2010, it was for sale through Pittsburgh's Urban Redevelopment Authority.

4. Carnegie Library of Pittsburgh, Main

4400 Forbes Avenue, Oakland
Longfellow, Alden & Harlow (Boston and Pittsburgh), architects
for original building, 1892–95; Alden & Harlow, architects for
Forbes Avenue addition, 1899–1907
Carnegie Library and Institute: National Register of Historic Places;
City of Pittsburgh Historic District; Historic Landmark Plaque

After dropping out of Gladstone High School around his sixteenth birthday, August Wilson continued his education on his own informally at the main Carnegie Library in Oakland, where, he later said, it seemed that "they had all the books in the world."

Conceived by Andrew Carnegie as a cultural palace for the people, this building originally housed a library, art museum, natural history museum, and concert hall. In 1897, just two years after the Carnegie Library and Institute opened, Carnegie authorized its enlargement, which was completed in 1907.

5. Soldiers and Sailors Memorial Hall and Museum

4141 Fifth Avenue
Henry Hornbostel, Palmer & Hornbostel (New York), architects, 1907–10
National Register of Historic Places; City of Pittsburgh Historic Structure;
Historic Landmark Plaque

August Wilson planned most of the details of his funeral, and in implementing his wishes, his widow, Constanza Romero, arranged for it to be held in the assembly hall of Soldiers and Sailors on October 8, 2005. Designed to evoke the Mausoleum of Halicarnassus (erected in 377 B.C. as the tomb of King Mausolus and one of the Seven Wonders of the ancient world), Soldiers and Sailors was originally built to honor Civil War veterans. The text of Abraham Lincoln's Gettysburg Address is painted on the wall above the stage. This and other Civil War memorials provided a moving context for the life of this dramatist of racial division and healing.

This monumental building was rededicated in 1963 to honor all veterans. It is one of the earliest and most prominently sited of the "City Beautiful" structures erected in Pittsburgh's Oakland Civic Center Historic District. The architect, Henry Hornbostel, designed some fifty buildings in Pittsburgh and

established its first School of Architecture at what is now
Carnegie Mellon University.

6. Central Catholic High School

4720 Fifth Avenue, Oakland
Edward J. Weber of Link, Weber & Bowers, architect, 1926–27
Historic Landmark Plaque

August Wilson attended Central Catholic in 1959-60. It is
the leading Roman Catholic boy's school in Pittsburgh, but
as Wilson recalled, there was hardly a day when he was not
physically bullied and taunted with racist epithets. A group
picture of his section of the ninth grade in the Central Catholic
yearbook shows him as the only African American and the
only student with his head down, not looking at the camera.
The school principal and Wilson's English teacher were sup-
portive, though. Wilson recalled, "Brother Dominic ... would
always tell me I could be an author, and I needed to hear that."

The building was designed by Edward Weber, best known
for his ecclesiastical buildings which were, like Central
Catholic, inspired by French Gothic architecture. Weber also
designed several outstanding Art Deco public schools, including Mifflin (1932), Lemington (1937), and Schiller (1939).

7. 5822 Alder Street

Between Maryland Avenue and College Street, Shadyside

For *The Piano Lesson*, the only Pittsburgh Cycle play that has been filmed, August Wilson wrote the screenplay, shortening his text by more than a third. The play is set in Doaker Charles' home, somewhere in the Hill District, but for exterior shots in the 1995 *Hallmark Hall of Fame* television movie, Alder Street, suitably stocked with period automobiles, stood in for the 1936 Hill. Other Pittsburgh locations used in the film include the Garden Theater on the Northside, with its pornography posters changed for the occasion, where Boy Willie and Lymon meet Grace and a friend; Squirrel Hill, where they go to sell watermelons; and the Union Trust Building, downtown, standing in for the Gulf Building, where Avery works as an elevator operator.

8. New Hazlett Theater

Allegheny Center, Northside
Smithmeyer & Pelz (Washington, D.C.), architects, 1888–90
Sylvester Damianos, renovation architect, 1974
Entire building: National Register of Historic Places; City of Pittsburgh Historic Structure; Historic Landmark Plaque

The New Hazlett Theater is home to a variety of theater, dance, and music performances. August Wilson knew the New Hazlett under its former name, the Pittsburgh Public Theater, established here in 1974; the theater was named after Theodore L. Hazlett, Jr., in 1980. In 1976 Wilson attended a performance here of Athol Fugard's *Sizwe Bansi Is Dead*, a drama of a black man trying to find his identity under South African apartheid. It was the first, fully professional play that

impressed Wilson. In a 1987 interview with David Savran, he said, "I thought, 'This is great. I wonder if I could write something like this?'"

In 1996, Wilson returned to the Pittsburgh Public Theater and the Hazlett to revise *Jitney* for its professional rebirth. (In an earlier version, it had premiered in 1982—the first of the Pittsburgh Cycle plays—at the Allegheny Repertory Theatre in Pittsburgh's Oakland neighborhood.)

The Hazlett was originally the Carnegie Music Hall, part of the Northside branch of the Carnegie Library, originally the Carnegie Library of Allegheny City. This was the first Carnegie library commissioned in the United States by Andrew Carnegie; it was designed by the architects of the Library of Congress. In 2010, the library part of the building was being used as a storage facility for the Carnegie Library of Pittsburgh.

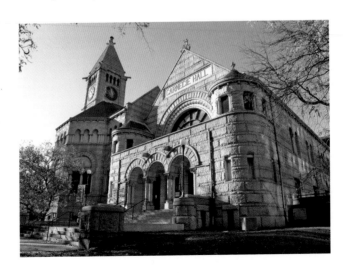

9. O'Reilly Theater (Pittsburgh Public Theater)

621 Penn Avenue, Downtown
Michael Graves (Princeton, NJ), architect, 1999, and Theater Square,
with WTW, associated architects, 2003

The O'Reilly opened on December 9, 1999, as the new home of the Pittsburgh Public Theater, with the premiere of August Wilson's *King Hedley II*. Wilson was so pleased to have the honor of opening this handsome new theater in his hometown that he delayed the play's completion for a year.

The Pittsburgh Cultural Trust commissioned the 650-seat theater, along with the adjoining Theater Square (containing a 250-seat cabaret theater, centralized box office, satellite studio for WQED-FM, restaurant, and parking garage) and Agnes R. Katz Plaza.

10. August Wilson Center for African American Culture

980 Liberty Avenue, Downtown
Allison Williams for Perkins + Will (San Francisco Office, CA),
architect, 2009

Originally, August Wilson had agreed to be honorary chairman of this long-planned center, designed as a showcase for African American arts in the Cultural District. When Wilson died suddenly during the planning of the project, his widow, Constanza Romero, gave the Center permission to honor his name. In its inaugural season, the Center hosted productions over two weeks in November 2009 of what it called the Aunt Ester Cycle of plays. The cycle featured St. Louis Black

Repertory in *Gem of the Ocean*; Pittsburgh Playwrights Theatre in *Two Trains Running*; St. Paul's Penumbra Theatre in *Radio Golf*; performance symposiums on *King Hedley II*; along with panel discussions and *The Women of the Hill*, a program of oral history arranged by Ping Chong and Talvin Wilks. The mission of the Center is to engage regional and national audiences in preserving, presenting, interpreting, celebrating, and shaping the art, culture, and history of African Americans in Western Pennsylvania and people of African descent throughout the world. The facility includes a 486-seat theater, seven exhibition galleries, a dance/theater space, and a cultivation center for classes, lectures, and hands-

on learning. Works by famed photographer Charles "Teenie" Harris (1908–98) and sculptor Thaddeus Mosley (b. 1926) are part of the Center's permanent collection.

11. Allegheny County Courthouse and Former Jail

436 Grant Street, Downtown
Henry Hobson Richardson (Brookline, MA), architect, 1884–88
National Historic Landmark; Historic Landmark Plaque

The jail or courthouse mentioned in more than half of the Pittsburgh Cycle plays is most likely this one. The following exchange is from *King Hedley II*:

> MISTER: He [King] said he was going down to the courthouse. Hop was having his hearing today to see if they was gonna give him the contract.
> TONYA: I hope he don't go down there acting a fool. I know King. He liable to go down there and cuss out the judge.

Between 1999 and 2001, the Jail was renovated to house the Family Division of the Allegheny County Court of Common Pleas, and a new jail was built along the Monongahela River. H. H. Richardson's massive granite Courthouse and former Jail remain Pittsburgh's most significant buildings. They became a prototype for late-19th-century civic and correctional facilities throughout the United States and Canada.

12. State Correctional Institution at Pittsburgh

3001 Beaver Avenue, Marshall-Shadeland
E. M. Butz, architect, 1876–82

This facility, originally the Western State Penitentiary, opened in 1882 and is Pennsylvania's oldest operating correctional institution. The penitentiary is mentioned in a number of August Wilson's plays, including *Jitney*:

> TURNBO: You don't know about Becker's son?
> YOUNGBLOOD: Know what?
> TURNBO: Becker's boy been in the penitentiary for twenty years. He's getting out today.
> YOUNGBLOOD: I ain't even knew Becker had a son.
> TURNBO: Been in the penitentiary for twenty years!
> Right down there at the Western State Pen, and Becker ain't never been down there to see him once!

Impressively sited along the Ohio River about five miles west of downtown Pittsburgh, the Western Penitentiary closed in January 2005 but reopened in June 2007 as the State Correctional Institution at Pittsburgh to house inmates needing substance abuse treatment.

13. Greenwood Cemetery

321 Kittanning Pike, O'Hara Township
Incorporated 1874

Located in O'Hara Township, about six miles northeast of downtown Pittsburgh, Greenwood is a well-established regional cemetery and the final resting place for August Wilson. It was once one of the few area cemeteries that would accept African Americans, along with indigents for whom the City of Pittsburgh paid a minimal burial charge.

Wilson's mother, Daisy, and maternal grandmother, Zonia, were buried here, their graves marked only with numbers, until Wilson, once he became successful, paid for proper markers. Floyd makes a similar arrangement for his departed mother in *Seven Guitars*.

> RED CARTER: Where your mother buried at, Floyd? My uncle's out in Greenwood.
> FLOYD: That's where she at. She out there in Greenwood. I was out there today. Me and Canewell went out there. ...
> Said I was gonna get her a marker. And that's what I'm

A black granite headstone marks August Wilson's grave in Section 7 of Greenwood Cemetery. He died on October 2, 2005 in Seattle and was buried here on October 8.

gonna do. Because when I leave this time I ain't planning on coming back. I get her that marker and I won't owe nobody nothing.

Wilson chose to be buried here, and in accord with his wishes, the front of his tombstone reads, along with his name and birth and death years,

Playwright
Poet
Loving Husband, Father
Brother, Friend
"Wherever You Are
You Are
I'm Here"

Appendices

August Wilson in the backyard of 1621 Bedford Avenue (see page 68). This was the last residence of his mother, Daisy. On the visit in 1999 pictured here, Wilson said that this backyard inspired the set for *King Hedley II*.

The Pittsburgh Cycle: Summaries

Christopher Rawson

August Wilson's ten-play, century-long epic focuses on challenges characteristic of each decade. But it also looks back to slavery and to two great, wrenching diasporas. The first is the fearsome middle passage of the slave ships and the mid-Atlantic City of Bones, apocalyptic testimony to the human cost of the slave trade and the spiritual burden and inspiration passed to its descendants. The second is the successive post-Civil War waves of black migration from the agrarian South to the industrial North, represented by Pittsburgh and Wilson's native Hill District.

In response to those cataclysmic diasporas, a recurring theme throughout the cycle is a resourceful people's sense of destiny and each individual's "song"—the sense of a personal, spiritual relationship to that shared past. Being cut off from that song, as with Levee in *Ma Rainey's Black Bottom* or the title character in *King Hedley II*, continues that wrenching past into a tragic present. But finding that individual song can turn past and present into a hopeful future—that is what *Joe Turner's Come and Gone* is ultimately all about. For Wilson himself, that hopeful song was found in theater, which, as he memorably said, beckoned him down "a road which has welcomed me with fresh endearments and sprouted yams and bolls of cotton at my footfall."

In most of the plays there are characters who embody that legacy of past suffering and hard-won wisdom. Chief among these is the semi-mythic Aunt Ester (say it aloud: it sounds like *an-cestor*), a shaman and healer. Although Wilson did not create her until he wrote his fifth Pittsburgh Cycle play, *Two Trains Running*, she appears on- or off-stage in three more plays. He later called her the cycle's central character. She is said to have been born in 1619, the year the first Africans arrived in

Virginia, but we eventually realize that hers is a hereditary function, passed down from generation to generation.

In *Two Trains Running* (set in 1969, staged on Broadway in 1992), Ester offers off-stage hope to one of Wilson's young men seeking a viable future. We next hear of her in *King Hedley II* (set in 1985, on Broadway in 2001), where her death marks a tragic low in the hopes of African America. The only time we see her in the flesh is in *Gem of the Ocean* (set in 1904, on Broadway in 2004), when her house at 1839 Wylie Avenue is a sanctuary for veterans of the old underground railroad and a command post for opposition to the new slavery of company store, kickbacks to employers, and racist unions. Her spirit returns to life in *Radio Golf* (set in 1997, on Broadway in 2007), in which an urban redevelopment scheme threatens to dishonor the history embodied in her house.

For the following brief summaries, the ten plays are listed in the order of the years in which they take place, creating the century-long panorama that is part of Wilson's grand design. The second date is when each play was first staged in New York, at which point Wilson considered it finished. But students of the Pittsburgh Cycle may consider this order of composition the more important one: *Ma Rainey's Black Bottom, Fences, Joe Turner's Come and Gone, The Piano Lesson, Two Trains Running, Seven Guitars, Jitney, King Hedley II, Gem of the Ocean,* and *Radio Golf.*

All the plays but *Ma Rainey* mention many Pittsburgh places; a selection is featured in the Guide (pages 57–117).

Gem of the Ocean, 1904 (2004)

Into Aunt Ester's house on Wylie Avenue comes a young man, Citizen Barlow, seeking to have his soul washed of guilt. He is nurtured by Aunt Ester (memorably played on Broadway by Phylicia Rashad); mentored by elderly veterans of the Civil War and the underground railroad; menaced by Caesar Wilks, a black sheriff who serves the white mill owners as a latter-day overseer; and intrigued by Black Mary, Ester's apprentice healer. The turbulent twentieth century is launched and the torch of resistance is passed.

See Aunt Ester's House, pages 76–79.

Joe Turner's Come and Gone, 1911 (1988)

Seth and Bertha Holly's boarding house is a temporary haven for African Americans moving northward to find a new life or to search for family members lost under the oppression of sharecropping and chain gangs. Bynum Walker, the shaman or wise man of the play, speaks of the "binding song" which can put African Americans in touch with their destinies, and he presides over a celebratory "juba" that unleashes Herald Loomis's terrifying vision of the City of Bones.

See 1600 Block Webster Avenue/Manilla Street, page 72.

Ma Rainey's Black Bottom, 1927 (1984)

While the white agent and studio boss wait angrily in a Chicago recording studio for blues star Ma Rainey to show up for her recording date, the four musicians in her band rehearse and bicker, tell stories and dream. Tensions rise, especially for Levee, the hopeful trumpet player, with tragic results. In this first Wilson play to reach New York, both the playwright and his first angry young man (played by Charles Dutton in an electric Broadway debut) issue their challenge to America. Dutton also starred in the 2003 Broadway revival with Whoopi Goldberg.

Asked why *Ma Rainey* is the only play not set in Pittsburgh, Wilson said of his first breakthrough play, "I was from Pittsburgh, so I thought I needed a more important city." But there is no doubt its picture of black musicians is imaginatively based on the active music scene he experienced in his native Hill District.

The Piano Lesson, 1936 (1990)

The most precious possession of the Charles family is an upright piano. When they were slaves to the Sutter family in 1856, a Charles child and his mother were traded for the piano, and the child's father carved his grief on it in scenes of family history. Years later, his descendants stole the piano back and lives were lost. Now it is the focal point in a struggle between two Charles descendants, Boy Willie and Berniece, over how to use this painful legacy. Berniece wants to keep the piano intact and untouched, but her brother, Boy Willie, wants to sell it to buy the land on which the family had been slaves. Other family members get involved and the angry ghost of a Sutter arrives to have his say.

The setting is Berniece and Doaker Charles's house in the Hill. The only clue to its location is that Berniece takes young Maretha on a streetcar and drops her at the Irene Kaufmann Settlement House (now Hill House) on the way downtown, so it must be east of there. When *Piano Lesson* was filmed in Pittsburgh in 1994 for television's *Hallmark Hall of Fame,* Shadyside's Alder Street stood in for the Hill of 1936. Charles Dutton reprised his Broadway performance as Boy Willie, joined by Alfre Woodard as Berniece.

See 5822 Alder Street, page 110.

Seven Guitars, 1948 (1996)

Floyd Barton is a returned veteran in the expansive atmosphere after World War II. A natural musician with one hit song, he dreams of the big time and longs to return to the Chicago music scene. But as the play begins, Vera and Floyd's friends mourn his death. In Wilson's only play constructed in flashback, we go back to discover who killed Floyd Barton and, more importantly, to explore why he died and under the pressure of what issues, emotions, and history, both personal and communal.

See 1727 Bedford Avenue, pages 70–71.

Fences, 1957–58 and 1963 (1987)

The most popular play of the cycle, a record money-maker on Broadway with towering performances by James Earl Jones and Mary Alice, *Fences* was successfully revived in 2010 with Denzel Washington and Viola Davis. It is often likened to Arthur Miller's *Death of a Salesman*, which it partly resembles. But unlike Miller's Willie Loman, Wilson's Troy Maxson is bigger than life. He was a Negro League baseball star who spent many years in jail; now he's a trash collector fighting for blacks to be allowed to drive as well as haul. Opposing him is his teenage son, hopeful of something better, while his wife Rose, older son, brother, and friend bear complex testimony.

See 1712 Bedford Avenue, page 69.

Two Trains Running, 1969 (1992)

In the aftermath of the 1968 riots following the assassination of Martin Luther King, Jr., and in the heyday of black power, a bumptious young man named Sterling arrives at Memphis's diner to learn his way around the Hill. He also checks out Risa, a pretty waitress who has scarred herself in protest against being hit on for sex. The deranged Hambone seeks the ham he was promised for a painting job, refusing to settle for a chicken, while Memphis battles with the city, which wants to underpay him for his land. The resident philosopher is Holloway, but in the background there is the ancient seer Aunt Ester, whom Sterling (played on Broadway by Laurence Fishburne) hopes to see. Surprisingly, Wilson's 1960s play is his least angry and most compassionate.

See Eddie's Restaurant, pages 83–84.

Jitney, 1977 (original version staged in Pittsburgh in 1982; rewritten for New York debut, 2000)

Out of a scruffy jitney station in the Hill, Becker and four others hustle to make a living driving places licensed cabs will not go. In between calls, they gossip and bicker with each other and the neighborhood numbers runner. Then Becker's son arrives, freed from a long jail term for a murder based on passionate principle, and the central conflict between father and son develops. But it is the by-play among the men that makes this such a richly comic, audience-friendly play.

See Westbrook Jitney Station, page 81.

King Hedley II, 1985 (2001)

The quasi-Shakespearean title is justified by the most darkly tragic play of the Pittsburgh Cycle. Hedley was named King for his supposed father (the strange West Indian in *Seven Guitars*), by his mother Ruby, a young woman in that same play. Now, King is a tragic figure of size and passion who struggles to earn respect and carve out a life in a dusty Hill backyard, like a town square in an ancient Greek tragedy. Offstage, the ancient Aunt Ester dies, King's plans go awry, and his family heritage, in the figure of Elmore, his mother's one-time lover, rises up to challenge his sense of self.

See 1621 Bedford Avenue, page 68, and photo on page 120.

Radio Golf, 1997 (2007)

In Wilson's only play to be set among the black bourgeoisie, Harmond Wilks is in the running to be Pittsburgh's first black mayor, while simultaneously planning a bold redevelopment deal. His wife, Mame, and friend, Roosevelt Hicks, encourage him. Scheduled to be torn down is 1839 Wylie Avenue, the mansion that was once Aunt Ester's. The historical connection with her has been lost, but then Elder Joseph Barlow appears, reviving the Barlow-Wilks relationship from *Gem of the Ocean*. He joins Sterling Johnson, twenty-eight years older than he was in *Two Trains Running*, to urge Harmond to reconnect with his people. The battle between money and values is joined once more.

The setting is Harmond's real estate redevelopment office, somewhere in the Hill's Centre Avenue business district.

Looking north toward Centre Avenue from Elmore Street near Rose
Street. Rose is a central character in *Fences,* and Elmore is a central
character in *King Hedley II.* Notice Lutz's Meat Market at the bottom
of Elmore on Centre Avenue, and Crawford Grill No. 2 beyond on
Wylie Avenue. The two buildings are on either side of the telephone
poles. Construction equipment is on the site of the Thelma Lovette
Family YMCA, under construction in 2010–11.

Webster Avenue looking west: the U.S. Steel Building of 1971 is Pittsburgh's tallest skyscraper and the Gulf Building of 1932 is to its right, just visible above a cluster of houses in the Hill District.

Acknowledgments

Louise King Sturgess

How a book develops from an initial concept to a published work is a story in itself. With two of our African American publications out of print—*A Legacy in Bricks and Mortar: African-American Landmarks in Allegheny County* and *The African-American Legacy in Allegheny County: A Timeline of Key Events*—we recognized the need to publish a new book building on scholarly research and survey efforts by the Pittsburgh History & Landmarks Foundation (PHLF).

With the opening of the August Wilson Center for African American Culture and a federal matching grant program offered through the Pennsylvania Historical and Museum Commission for "preserving and interpreting African American Heritage in Pennsylvania," we knew it would be useful to publish a guidebook to a selection of sites associated with the life and work of Pittsburgh-born playwright August Wilson. This would be the fourth guidebook in a PHLF series, following on the publication of the *Allegheny County Courthouse and Jail Walking Tour* (2007), *Whirlwind Walk: Architecture and Urban Spaces in Downtown Pittsburgh* (2008), and *Charles J. Connick: His Education and His Windows in and near Pittsburgh* (2008).

August Wilson: Pittsburgh Places in His Life and Plays makes Wilson's life and work more accessible to the public and encourages people to read his plays and to care for, respect, and preserve the Pittsburgh places connected with his legacy. Based on interviews with the playwright, the plays themselves, and historical research, this guidebook promotes "greater shared knowledge about the nation's past," strengthens "regional identities and local pride," and helps increase "local participation in preserving the country's cultural and natural heritage"—all stated goals of the Preserve America African American Initiative Grant.

The Multicultural Arts Initiative gave PHLF a lead grant for this project. BNY Mellon Foundation of Southwestern Pennsylvania generously contributed matching funds so PHLF could secure a grant from the Pennsylvania Historical and Museum Commission. Howard B. Slaughter, Jr., helped formulate the project concept and also made a donation to the guidebook. PHLF member Harry C. Goldby provided funding support for photography, and many other members made generous donations, too.

Most of all, we are deeply grateful to the authors, Laurence A. Glasco and Christopher Rawson, who embraced this project from the outset and worked closely with our staff in every way. Mr. Glasco thanks Lillian Allen, John Brewer, Alma Speed Fox, Fred Logan, Thelma Lovette, Ralph Proctor, Sala Udin, and others from the Hill District who shared their stories and knowledge with him. Christopher Rawson thanks the many dozens of August Wilson interpreters—actors, directors, designers, critics, and scholars, both local and national—as well as Wilson family members and friends with whom he has talked or conducted interviews over the past twenty-five years. Thanks also to the students in his University of Pittsburgh courses on August Wilson who have deepened his understanding of the plays. Special thanks to Bill Wade and other *Pittsburgh Post-Gazette* photographers, and to Constanza Romero, Todd Kreidler, and Dena Levitin. Many ideas and portions of text used in this book appeared originally in material written by Mr. Rawson for the *Pittsburgh Post-Gazette* and are reprinted here with permission.

We thank Kimberly C. Ellis of Historic Hill Institute and Sala Udin of Coro Center for Civic Leadership for their contributions and thoughtful review of the manuscript. The following people also provided constructive comments and edits: Terri Baltimore, Hill House Association; Laurie J. Cohen, Hillman Library; André Kimo Stone Guess, August Wilson Center for African American Culture; Philip B. Hallen, Falk Foundation;

The Rhumba Theater, c. 1957. Doaker tells Lymon about the Rhumba in *The Piano Lesson*: "Right down there on Fullerton Street. Can't miss it. Got the speakers outside on the sidewalk. You can hear it a block away."

Matthew G. Hyland, Duquesne University; and Robert M. Lavelle, Lavelle Real Estate, Inc. Sister Margery Kundar, CSJ, principal of St. Benedict the Moor School, provided information about August Wilson's years as a student at Holy Trinity and St. Richard's schools and about Wilson's visit to St. Benedict the Moor School in 1989.

At PHLF, Albert M. Tannler, historical collections director, compiled the bibliography and provided essential research and writing assistance for the sites in the guidebook. Frank Stroker, assistant archivist, and Anne Nelson, general counsel, provided valuable research support. I also thank Jack Miller, Mary Lu Denny, Marie Miller, and Karen Cahall for their help. Many college interns also provided assistance, including Jennifer Ayers, Lynley Bernstein, Melanie Haake, Amanda Leonard, Megan Poset, William Prince, and Kyra Zemanick.

Greg Pytlik of Pytlik Design Associates, Inc. and Beth Buckholtz worked patiently with us to produce a handy, educational guidebook. All in all, a team effort by many.

Illustration Sources

Opposite: The 2100 block of Wylie Avenue, near Kirkpatrick Street. Wylie is referenced in six of the nine plays August Wilson set in Pittsburgh's Hill: most importantly, he imagined Aunt Ester's house at 1839 Wylie. Wylie was once said to be the only street in America that began at a church and ended at a jail. John Wesley A.M.E. Zion is still sited at the eastern end of Wylie. The Allegheny County Courthouse and former Jail remain at the western end, although Wylie no longer ends there due to street-grid changes in the 1950s.

Bibliography (chronological order)

I. August Wilson

Complete Plays

Wilson, August. *The August Wilson Century Cycle*. Series Introduction by John Lahr. New York: Theatre Communications Group, 2007.

Writings by and about August Wilson

Shannon, Sandra D. *The Dramatic Vision of August Wilson*. Washington: Howard University Press, 1995.

Brantley, Ben. Interview about TV version of *The Piano Lesson*. *New York Times*, 1 February 1995.

Wilson, August. *The Ground on Which I Stand*. New York: Theatre Communications Group, 2001.

Wilson, August. *Conversations with August Wilson*. Ed. by Jackson R. Bryer and Mary E. Hartig. Jackson, MS: University Press of Mississippi, 2006.

Pittsburgh Post-Gazette: Aside from *Conversations with August Wilson* (above), the largest collection of interviews with Wilson is in the archive of his hometown newspaper, which covered him and his work thoroughly since the debut of *Jitney* at the Allegheny Repertory Theatre in 1982. Included are far too many interviews, features, theatrical previews, reviews, column items, commentaries, and pieces by Wilson himself to list, but a few follow.

The best place to start is the *Post-Gazette* website, www.post-gazette.com. Some coverage is gathered on an August Wilson Index page, reachable from the Theater page (www.post-gazette.com/theater; scroll down on left) or directly at http://www.post-gazette.com/pg/03001/497623.stm. Much of the coverage since 1998 is still online.

Wilson, August. Accepting Pittsburgher of the Year honor, 27 January 1990.

Wilson, August. Talk at Pitt's Honor Convocation, 21 March 1992.

A stool from Eddie's Restaurant (see pages 83–84) has been installed in the Carnegie Library of Pittsburgh's Hill District branch, 2177 Centre Avenue. Markers on the 1923 map of the Hill identify the conjectured locations of Wilson's plays.

Wilson, August. Talk at Carnegie Library, 28 March 1999.

Wilson. August. Lecture at Heinz series, 21 March 2000.

Wilson, August. Heinz Award acceptance speech, 4 December 2003.

Rawson, Christopher. Interviews (selected) with August Wilson: 16 November 1991; 10 June 1996; 26 April 1997; 24 March 1998; 18 March 1999; 6 April 1999; 5 December 1999; 5 July 2001; 8 February 2003; 6 December 2003; 7 December 2004; 26 August 2005.

Rawson, Christopher. Interview with West family about *Two Trains Running*, 2 August 1994.

Rawson, Christopher. Interview with Constanza Romero, 25 June 1996.

II. The Hill

The *African American Historic Sites Survey of Allegheny County* (completed 1992; published PHMC 1994) was a pioneering identification and assessment of black historical sites in Allegheny County. Between 1992 and 2010 further research has uncovered omissions and factual errors, understandably. Some errors have been repeated in later publications, including the widely distributed *A Legacy in Bricks and Mortar* (PHLF 1995) and "Discover the Legacy: The African American Experience in Southwestern Pennsylvania—A Historic Tour" (YPAP 2010). When known, any errors have been corrected in the text of this guidebook.

Society/Culture/Entertainment

The *Pittsburgh Courier* 1910-1965; *New Pittsburgh Courier* 1966–present. The *Courier* has been digitized (1911–2002) and may be searched at http://pqasb.pqarchiver.com/pittsburghcourier/advancedsearch.html.

The Jewish Criterion. "Irene Kaufmann Settlement: New Building Formally Dedicated Last Sunday," 32:9 (April 7, 1911): 3–5; "To Enlarge Irene Kaufmann Settlement Through Generous Gift of Henry Kaufmann," 71:24 (March 20, 1928): 57; "Hendel Enterprises," 72:16 (August 24, 1928): 23; "The Hendel Theater Corporation," 73:15 (February 15, 1929): 20; "New Roosevelt Theatre Opened," 73:15 (February 15, 1929): 20. *The Jewish Criterion* (1895–1962) is available online at http://pjn.library.cmu.edu/

Reid, Ira DeAugustine, et al. *Social Conditions of the Negro in the Hill District of Pittsburgh.* Pittsburgh: General Committee on the Hill Survey, 1930.

"City Awaits the Savoy Ballroom Opening." *Pittsburgh Courier*, 23 December 1933.

"Huge Crowd Turns Out for Opening of New Granada Theater." *Pittsburgh Courier*, 22 May 1937.

Glasco, Laurence A. "Double Burden: The Black Experience in Pittsburgh," *City at the Point: Essays on the Social History of Pittsburgh*, ed. by Samuel P. Hays. Pittsburgh: University of Pittsburgh Press, 1989: 69–109.

Lubove, Roy. *Twentieth Century Pittsburgh: Government, Business, and Environmental Change*, Vol. 1, Pittsburgh: University of Pittsburgh Press, 1995.

Fullilove, Mindy Thompson. *Root Shock: How Tearing Up City Neighborhoods Hurts America, and What We Can Do About It.* New York: Random House, 2004.

Glasco, Laurence A., ed. *The WPA History of the Negro in Pittsburgh.* Pittsburgh: University of Pittsburgh Press, 2004.

Brewer, John M., Jr., *African Americans in Pittsburgh.* Charleston, SC: Arcadia, 2006.

Burstin, Barbara S. *Steel City Jews: A History of Pittsburgh and Its Jewish Community 1840–1915.* Apollo, Pa.: Closson Press, 2008.

Trotter, Joe W., and Jared N. Day. *Race and Renaissance: African Americans in Pittsburgh since World War II.* Pittsburgh: University of Pittsburgh Press, 2010.

Young Preservationist Association of Pittsburgh. "Discover the Legacy: The African American Experience in Southwestern Pennsylvania—A Historic Tour." 2010.

Architecture

"Knights of Pythias Temple, Pittsburgh." *Buildings of Character Erected by Hodder Construction Co., Inc., Braddock, Pa.* Braddock: Daily News Herald, n.d.: [20].

"K. of P.'s to Erect $300,000 Temple; Drawing of Architect Approved." *Pittsburgh Courier,* 12 March 1927, 1, 8.

"Many Witness Corner-Stone Laying of Pythian Temple." *Pittsburgh Courier*, 31 March 1928, 11.

Harmon Foundation. *Negro Artists: An Illustrated Review of Their Achievements.* New York: Harmon Foundation, 1935: 43.

McMullen, Leo A. "Architecture in the Diocese." *Catholic Pittsburgh's One Hundred Years*. Chicago: Loyola University Press, 1943: 186–200. [Digitized on Historic Pittsburgh: http://digital.library.pitt.edu/pittsburgh]

Cederholm, Theresa Dickason. *Afro-American Artists: A Biobibliographical Directory*. Boston: Boston Public Library, 1973: 22.

Brown, Eliza Smith, et al. *African American Historic Sites Survey of Allegheny County*. Harrisburg: Pennsylvania Historical and Museum Commission, 1994.

Bolden, Frank E., Laurence A. Glasco, and Eliza Smith Brown. *A Legacy in Bricks and Mortar: African-American Landmarks in Allegheny County*. Pittsburgh: Pittsburgh History & Landmarks Foundation, 1995.

Kidney, Walter C. *Pittsburgh's Landmark Architecture: The Historic Buildings of Pittsburgh and Allegheny County*. Pittsburgh: Pittsburgh History & Landmarks Foundation, 1997.

Falk, Peter Hastings, ed. "Louis A. S. Bellinger." *Who Was Who in American Art 1564–1975*. Madison, CT: Sound View Press, 1999: Vol. 1: 271.

Tannler, Albert M. "Louis Arnett Stewart [*sic*] Bellinger (1891–1946)." *African American Architects: A Biographical Dictionary 1865–1945*. Edited by Dreck Spurlock Wilson. New York: Routledge, 2004: 30–32.

Zurier, Sarah H. "Walter Lennox Roberts, Jr. (1908–1982)." *African American Architects: A Biographical Dictionary 1865–1945*. Edited by Dreck Spurlock Wilson. New York: Routledge, 2004: 347–350.

Pfaffmann + Associates. "August Wilson House: Historic Structure Report & Feasibility Study for August Wilson Center for African American Culture and Paul A. Ellis Jr. and Family" (Pittsburgh, December 2008).

Strecker, Geri. "The Rise and Fall of Greenlee Field," *Black Ball* 2:2 (Fall 2009): 37–67.

Tannler, Albert M. "Pittsburgh's African-American Architect Louis Bellinger and the New Granada Theater." (2010) www.phlf.org

Donnelly, Lu, H. David Brumble IV, and Franklin Toker. *Buildings of Pennsylvania: Pittsburgh and Western Pennsylvania*. Charlottesville and London: University of Virginia Press in association with the Society of Architectural Historians, 2010.

American Architects and Buildings: www.philadelphiabuildings.org

"Photo Gallery and List of Parishes in the Diocese by County and Founding Date." Diocese of Pittsburgh Archives: www.diopitt.org/archives/archives.htm

Index

The titles of August Wilson's plays are in bold italics.

525 William Penn Place: x
1600 Block Webster Avenue/ Manilla Street: 58, 72
1621 Bedford Avenue: xiv, 58, 68, 83, 120
1710 Bedford Avenue: 58, 69
1712 Bedford Avenue: 58, 69
1725 Bedford Avenue: 31, 58, 69
1727 Bedford Avenue: ii, 2–3, 6, 20–21, 30, 31, 52, 58, 70–71
1839 Wylie Avenue (*see* Aunt Ester's House)
5822 Alder Street: 100, 110

A. Leo Weil (Pittsburgh Weil) School: 13, 58, 88–89
Albee, Edward: 6
Alcoa Building (1951–53): xx–1
Alden & Harlow (Longfellow, Alden & Harlow): 80, 104, 105, 107
Allegheny County Courthouse and Former Jail: 100, 114, 133
Allegheny Repertory Theatre: 15, 111
Allen, Lillian: 31
American Theatre Critics Association: 18, 22
Arcena Street: 58, 72, 73–74
August Wilson Center for African American Culture: 20, 100, 112–113
Aunt Ester's House: 56, 58, 76–79, 102, 133

Bambola, The: 32
Baraka, Amiri: xv, xix, 88

Bean, Herb: 32, 49
Bearden, Romare: xv
Bedford, David: 7
Bedford Dwellings: xviii, 34, 42, 52
Bell, Janet: 47
Bella's Market: 7, 30, 31, 70–71
Bellinger, Louis Arnett Stuart: 94–95
Benson, George: 53
Bickel, Charles: 98
Black Bart and the Sacred Hills: 14, 15
Black Horizon Theater: xix, 13, 42, 83, 88
Blakey, Art: 33, 53
Bolden, Frank E.: 38, 40
Borges, Jorge Luis: xv
Brady Street Bridge: 36
Brevard, Doris: 47
Brother Dominic: 109
Brown, Byrd: 42, 45, 46
Brown, Homer S.: 38
Brown, Lavera: 42
Brown, Leroy: 33
Brustein, Robert: 18
Bullins, Ed: 88
Burks, Dr. Charles: 46
Burley, Charlie: 69
Butera, Frank: 69
Butera, Johnny: 31, 69
Butz, E. M.: 115
Byrom, Fletcher: 46

Carnegie, Andrew: 7, 107, 111
Carnegie Library, Allegheny City: 111

Carnegie Library and Institute (Oakland): 17, 107

Carnegie Library of Pittsburgh, Main (Oakland): 9, 19, 100, 105, 107, 111, 144

Carnegie Library of Pittsburgh, Hazelwood (1900–2004): 8, 19, 100, 104–105

Carnegie Library of Pittsburgh, Hill District
1911 Wylie Avenue (1899–1982): 7, 19, 79, 80, 104
419 Dinwiddie Street (1982–2008): 23, 80, 146
2177 Centre Avenue (2008–): 32, 52, 59, 61, 84, 135

Carnegie Mellon University: 13, 88, 97, 98, 109

Carra, Lawrence: 13, 88

Central Catholic High School: 8, 9, 66, 100, 106, 109

Centre Avenue Poets Theater Workshop: 13, 91

Civic Arena (civic auditorium): vii, 26–27, 38, 39, 44, 54, 58, 63, 64

Clarke, Kenny: 33

Coldest Day of the Year, The: 14

Community Media: 17

Connelley Trade School (Clifford B.): 8, 58, 66–67, 106

Crawford Grill No. 2: 32, 52, 58, 82, 127

Crawford Square Apartments: 52, 65

Crawford Street (rented room): 10, 58, 65

Crawfords baseball team (*see* Pittsburgh Crawfords)

Daisy Wilson Artist Community, Inc.: 21

Damianos, Sylvester: 110

Daniel, Jack: 47

Dee, Mary: 33, 53

Degree, Sarah Miss: 8, 76

"Dingbat": 12

Dorow, John F. E.: 70

Duquesne University: 52

Dutton, Charles: 20

Ebenezer Tower (*see* Workingmen's Civic Club)

Eckstine, Billy: 53

Eddie's Restaurant: 12, 58, 60, 83–84, 135

Edmunds, Arthur J.: 46

Eldridge, Roy: 33

Ellis, Ed "Ewari": 91

Ellis, Paul A., Jr.: 20, 70

Ellis Hotel: 58, 90

Elmore Theater: 32

Epperson, David: 45

Eugene O'Neill Theater Center: 14–15

Everett, Sharry: 43

Falk, Gail: 42

Faulkner, William: 4

Fences: 4, 18, 20, 21, 36, 50, 61, 69, 82, 125, 127

First Muslim Mosque of Pittsburgh, The (*see also* Carnegie Library of Pittsburgh, Hill District, 1911 Wylie Avenue): 58, 79, 80

Flournoy, Nick: 12

Foggie, Bishop Charles: 34

Fox, Alma Speed: 42

Francis Street Community Garden and Urban Farm: 87

Freedom Corner Monument: 58, 62–63

Friel, Brian: 4

Fugard, Athol: 13, 110

Fullerton Street: 15, 63

Gallo, David: 5
Garner, Erroll: 53
Gem of the Ocean: vii, 36, 56, 73, 78, 106, 113, 122–123
Gibson, Josh: 88
Gladstone School: 9, 100, 106, 107
Goldblum, Dr. Raymond: 69
Gordon's Shoes: 32, 33
Graves, Howard K.: 62
Graves, Michael: 112
Greenlee, Gus: 53, 82
Greenlee Field: 85, 95
Greenwood Cemetery: 20, 100, 116–117
"Ground on Which I Stand, The": 18
Gulf Building (and Company): x–xi, 32, 110, 128

Haden, William "Bouie": 45
Halfway Art Gallery: 12, 58, 91
Hallen, Philip B.: 43, 49
Hardy, Thomas: 4
Harper, Walt: 53
Harris, Charles "Teenie": 32, 113, 133
Harris, Franco: 82
Heckert, Sidney F.: 87
Hill Arts Society: 12
Hill Community Development Corporation: 58, 92–93, 96
Hill House Association: 58, 61, 97–98, 99
Hines, Earl "Fatha": 33, 53
Hofer, Marguerite: 43
Holy Trinity R. C. Church and School: xvii, xviii, 8, 64
Homecoming: 14
Hornbostel, Henry: 108–109
Horne, Lena: 33
Howze, Sam (*see* Udin, Sala)
Humphries, Roger: 53

Ingham, Boyd & Pratt: 85
Irene Kaufmann Settlement (*see also* Kaufmann Auditorium): 97, 98–99
Irv's Bar: 92–93
Irvis, K. Leroy: 46, 48

Jackson, Billy: 17
Jackson, Clyde: 44, 49, 51
Jamal, Ahmad: 53
Janssen & Abbott: 85, 86
Jitney: x, 5, 14, 15, 17, 21, 22, 36, 41, 81, 83, 90, 92, 96–97, 98, 111, 115, 125–126
Joe Turner's Come and Gone: vii, xv, 21, 28, 36, 61, 69, 72, 96, 123
Johnson, Bob: 83
Jones, Paul: 38
Jones & Laughlin steel mill: 36, 37

Kaufmann Auditorium: 58, 98–99
Kennedy Center, Washington, D.C.: 22
King, Douglas: 47
King, Martin Luther, Jr.: 12, 48
King Hedley II: 17, 21, 22, 68, 75, 78, 82, 90, 93, 102, 112, 113, 114, 120, 126, 127
Kittel, Frederick August, Sr.: 6, 65, 71
Knox, Silas: 49
Kuntu Repertory Theatre: xix, 13, 17, 21

Lahr, John: 18
Lavelle, Robert M.: 43
Lavelle, Robert R.: 49, 51
Lee, Edward B.: 66
Legacy, The: 52, 53, 81
Letsche Education Center (School): 8, 58, 67, 89

Lewis, Dr. James: 46
Lillie, Dr. Vernell: xix, 13, 17
Link, A. F. & Associates: 104, 109
Loendi Club: 58, 72–73
Longfellow, Alden & Harlow
  (*see* Alden & Harlow)
Lovette, Thelma (*see also*
  Thelma Lovette Family
  YMCA): 31, 42
Lutz's Meat Market: 58, 83,
  89–90, 127

Ma Rainey's Black Bottom:
  3, 15, 16, 18, 20, 21, 61, 93, 123
Magasano, Dom: 32
Malcolm X: 43, 49, 95
Mann, Louise: 33
Marks, Alfred M.: 94, 95
Martin, Reverend Richard: 91
McClinton, Marion: 18, 22
McCoy, James, Jr.: 40, 44, 46, 49
McIlvane, Fr. Donald: 43
McKelvy School (*see* Miller
  African Centered Academy)
Mellon, E. P.: 85
Mellon Arena (*see* Civic Arena)
Miller, Arthur: 6
Miller African Centered
  Academy: 58, 75
Milliones, Jake: 42, 47, 62
Milliones, Margaret: 47
Milliones Manor: 86
Mitchell & Ritchey: 63
Moeser, Henry: 64, 76
Mordecai, Benjamin: 19–20
Morris, Carl: 48, 51
Moyers, Bill: 4, 22
Municipal Hospital of Infectious
  and Contagious Diseases:
  86–87

Neffke, Jan: 42
New Granada Theater (Pythian
  Temple): iv, 32, 43, 52, 58, 81,
  93, 94–96
New Hazlett Theater: 100,
  110–111
*New Pittsburgh Courier (see also
  Pittsburgh Courier)*: 33, 48

Ogot, Milton: 96
Oliver, Nathan: 11
O'Neill, Eugene: 6
O'Reilly Theater (*see also*
  Pittsburgh Public Theater):
  16, 17, 100, 112

Pace, Frankie: 40
Pat's Place: 10, 53
Peeler, Lawrence: 47
Pei, I. M.: 38, 63
Penn Incline: 73, 74
Penny, Rob: xix, 12, 13, 42, 43,
  81, 83, 88
Penumbra Theatre Company:
  14, 15, 113
Peterson, Carlos: 62
Pfaffmann + Associates: 84
Piano Lesson, The: x, xv, 17,
  20, 60, 61, 69, 83, 85, 98, 110,
  124, 131
Picovsky, Morris: 70
*Pittsburgh Courier, The (see also
  New Pittsburgh Courier)*: 32,
  33, 38, 89, 93
Pittsburgh Crawfords: 75, 82, 95
Pittsburgh Green Innovators: 67
Pittsburgh History & Landmarks
  Foundation: 61, 96, 103, 145
Pittsburgh Playwrights Theatre:
  21, 113
Pittsburgh Public Theater: 13,
  17, 21, 68, 100, 110–111, 112

Pittsburgh Weil School (*see* A. Leo Weil School)
Porter, Curtiss: 43
Pryor, William: 49
Purdy, Claude: xix, 14
Pythian Temple (*see* New Granada Theater)

Radio Golf: 5, 20, 41, 50, 52, 61, 77, 78, 97, 113, 126
Randolph, A. Philip: 44
Recycle: 14
Rhumba Theater: 32, 131
Richards, Lloyd: 4, 15
Richardson, Henry Hobson: 114
Roberts, Jr., Walter L.: 97–98
Robinson, Rev. Jimmy Joe: 44–45, 48
Robinson, Joseph: 82
Romero, Constanza: 16, 108, 112
Roosevelt Theater: 32
Rothschild Doyno Collaborative: 53

Safar, Dr. Peter: 49
St. Benedict the Moor Church: 40, 58, 64–65, 87
St. Benedict the Moor School (*see also* St. Richard's R. C. Church and School): 58, 87
St. Brigid's R. C. Church and School (St. Brigid Parish): 64, 65, 76, 79, 87
St. George Syrian/Antiochian Orthodox Church: 58, 68
St. Louis Black Repertory: 112–113
St. Paul, Minnesota: xix, 3, 14, 15, 23, 36, 113
St. Richard's R. C. Church and School (now St. Benedict the Moor School): xviii, 8, 65, 85, 87

St. Stephen's R. C. School and Church: 8, 100, 104
Sauer, Frederick C.: 104
Savoy Ballroom: 95
Savran, David: 111
Seattle, Washington: 3, 14, 16, 19, 20, 117
Seven Guitars: x, xx, 63, 69, 71, 73, 85, 92, 96, 116, 124
Shakespeare, William: 3
Shapira, Frieda: 42
Shrady, Frederick: 65
Siger, Beatrice (Bella): 30, 31, 70–71
Siger, Louis: 30, 31, 70
Sister Christopher: 87
Smith, Bessie: 12
Smith, Dr. Earl Belle: 46
Smith, Nate: 44
Smithmeyer & Pelz: 110, 111
Soldiers and Sailors Memorial Hall and Museum: 20, 100, 108–109
Stanley, William: 32
State Correctional Institution at Pittsburgh: 100, 115
Steen, Marion M.: 67, 88–89
Stotz, Edward: 98
Strayhorn, Billy: 33
Strong, Carlton: 75
Sullivan, Maxine: 33

Terrace Village: 34, 35, 52
Thelma Lovette Family YMCA: 52, 127
Thomas, Dylan: 11
Topp, O. M.: 106
Tuberculosis League Hospital Historic District: 58, 85–86
Turrentine, Stanley: 53

Two Trains Running: vii, x, 22, 36, 56, 68, 73, 78, 83, 85, 89, 90, 92, 95, 96, 113, 125

Udin, Sala: xvii–xix, 13, 42, 43, 62, 81, 83, 88, 91
Urban, Joseph: 99
Urban Design Associates: 65
Urban Redevelopment Authority of Pittsburgh: 38, 52, 63, 65, 106

Vann, Robert L.: 32, 33
Venson, Louis: 47
Vittor, Frank: 99

Washington, Milton: 49, 51
Washington Plaza Apartments: 38, 63
Weber, Edward J.: 109
West, Thomas L., Sr.: 84–85
West Funeral Home: 58, 83, 84–85
Westbrook Jitney Station: 58, 81
Western State Penitentiary (*see* State Correctional Institution at Pittsburgh)
Why I Learned to Read: 15

Williams, Allison, Perkins + Will: 112
Williams, Chawley: 12, 91
Williams, Rev. Elmer: 47
Williams, Mary Lou: 33, 53
Williams, Tennessee: 6
Williams, Vivian: 47
Wilson, August
  Kittel, Frederick August, Jr.: xvii, 6, 64, 70
  early family life: 6–7, 70–71
  siblings: 7, 71
  schooling: xvii, 8–9, 64, 66, 67, 85, 87, 104–107, 109
  changes name: 11, 65
  marriages: 12, 14, 16
  children: 12, 16
  on Broadway: 3, 4, 5, 15, 16, 18, 21, 122–126
  awards and honors: 6, 17, 18–19
Wilson, Daisy: xiv, xvii, 7, 21, 68, 71, 104, 106, 116, 120
Wilson, Zonia: 7, 69, 116
Workingmen's Civic Club (also Workmen's Club): 58, 96–97
Wylie Avenue: 12, 31, 33, 53, 56, 76–85, 95, 133

Yale Repertory Theatre: 15

An open book on the entrance door of the Carnegie Library of Pittsburgh in Oakland